間

SOCIAL
PRESENCING
THEATER

PI PRESS

CAMBRIDGE, MASSACHUSETTS

PI Press

Presencing Institute
1770 Massachusetts Avenue
Cambridge, MA 02140 USA
press@presencing.com

ISBN 978-0-9997179-7-4

Book design: Ricardo Dutra Goncalves and Kelvy Bird
Cover art: Japanese calligraphy of "ma" by Kobun Chino Otogawa

This book is dedicated to my precious Asher, Bea, and Opal,
whose natural true moves celebrate the goodness of this life.

CONTENTS

FOREWORD

BY OTTO SCHARMER

When I first met Arawana Hayashi, I was co-facilitating a workshop in Nova Scotia. The organizers of the conference had structured the event such that each workshop was paired up with a different team of artists each day. Arawana was one of them. On the day she joined our workshop, she introduced a practice called Duet, a type of explorative, meditative dance. In order to demonstrate the practice to the group, she needed a partner. She picked me. I don't think I had a choice (I probably would have tried to avoid that role).

What do I remember from that dance? Not much— except that it changed my life in less than five minutes. Within moments, I was in a different state of awareness and attention to what wanted to emerge from the "social field"—that is, from the quality of relationships that we have with each other, with ourselves, and with the unfolding situation.

In much of our lives our attention tends to be distracted by either the future or the past, by worrying about tomorrow or regretting things we did or didn't do yesterday. But in reality, there is only one access point for how we as humans actively participate in the unfolding of the universe: the now. Connecting to the now enables us to sense into the resonances of the past and the resonance of the future wanting to emerge.

If we assume that to be true, then the real question on the table is of course: How? How do we do that? How do we lean in to the current moment in a way that lets us sense the resonance of our highest future possibilities? How do we do that as individuals? How do we do that as a group? How do we do that as an organization or as a larger social system?

This book is all about the how. It lays out the foundations of a new discipline, a social art called Social Presencing Theater. Arawana has co-created this new social art-form—a set of methods and tools that change-makers worldwide are using to facilitate transformational change in their relationships, in their communities and organizations, in local and national government agencies, and in international institutions like the United Nations. This rapidly growing community of change-makers knows that to really change the outer world we first need to shift the inner place that we operate from, both as individuals and as communities.

Am I surprised to see the widespread adoption of this social-arts-based practice? No, not really. Its potential was evident right from the beginning when I first met Arawana. It just took a while to unfold, to manifest. And of course, it took a lot of work: by Arawana, and by the wonderful global core team of collaborators and co-creators that she convened and worked with over the years. Publishing this book is a key milestone on that still unfolding journey.

Publishing this book is also a key moment in the history of the Presencing Institute. Co-founded by Arawana, myself, and a small circle of colleagues who gathered in Boston in December 2005 during a blizzard, the Presencing Institute (PI) has taken root and is now co-held and co-shaped by a vibrant community of change-makers inspired by awareness-based systems change.

So what? Why does that matter?

Everyone knows that we live in a moment of profound disruption. It's a period of endings and beginnings. What's ending is a civilization focused on a way of operating that revolves around the ego. What wants to be born is a different civilization that is grounded in an awareness of the "eco"—that is, an awareness of the whole, the whole social field. As Arawana puts it so eloquently: "Social field awareness is the only paddle or rudder available to the small boat [of our current situation] as it moves out . . . into the unknown."

This book is about that rudder. It's a rudder that is available to each and every one of us. Social field awareness provides a practical rudder for guiding our boat—our communities—through periods of profound disruption and change as individuals, groups, organizations, and systems.

Today we know a lot about what is broken. We also know what we should be doing to reverse global warming and deal with hotspots of environmental and social breakdown and collapse. But are we doing those things? Mostly not. Instead, too often we collectively produce results that nobody wants. We say one thing, and we do another. So how can we address this disconnect between head and hand on the level of whole systems?

In my view there is only one way: It is by activating the intelligence of the heart. In this, the social arts are critical.

Social Presencing Theater is making a profound contribution to the evolution of systems thinking. It allows us to evolve the traditional state of the art of systems change by blending the methods and tools of systems thinking with those of systems sensing. Social Presencing Theater offers a new core methodology that over the past few years has become part of a new vocabulary for awareness-based systems change.

When I work with big organizations and institutions to bring about transformative innovation and change, why do I so often use the methods and tools of Social Presencing Theater? Because it's a very effective tool for helping a system sense and see itself. In other words, in a very short period of time, it shifts the conversation from debate to dialogue, it shifts the level of listening from shallow to deep, and it creates a new language that allows stakeholders to shift their quality of interaction from a silo to a systems view. In short, it helps change-makers to illuminate and work on some of the deeper structural blind spots and barriers that prevent the systems from naturally evolving.

At the core of all journeys of awareness-based systems change is something simple: a shift in the inner place from which we operate. It is a shift from the head to the heart, and from the heart to the hand—that is, to the whole body or system. The methods and tools of Social Presencing Theater provide a new social grammar that we need in order to decipher and address the new waves of disruption that are coming our way in the decades ahead.

Friedrich Nietzsche once suggested that his own task was "to look at science through the optic of the artist, but at art through the optic of life." That, in a nutshell, summarizes what at the Presencing Institute we aspire to do and what Arawana with her work on Social Presencing Theater has been pioneering for more than fifteen years.

"To look at science through the optic of the artist" means to deepen the scientific activity from looking at the world as it currently is to looking at the world as it emerges. And the only way of doing that is by integrating first-, second-, and third-person knowledge into the scientific inquiry. Which is precisely what Arawana describes in the closing chapters of the book.

"Through the optic of the artist" means from the perspective of the change-makers, not merely as onlookers. "Together with those near us and those around the planet," writes Arawana, "we co-create the societies in which we live. In this sense," she continues, echoing Joseph Beuys, "we are all social artists."

Perhaps this is one of the most profound ideas that this book brings into the world: that all of us are social artists who co-enact our global social sculpture—the sum total of all our relationships—moment to moment. Yet the way we do that often ignores the core principles that allow Social Presencing Theater practices to be so generative. Perhaps the most important one concerns the realignment of attention, intention, and behavior. Closing the feedback loop among those three elements is like applying the rudder, or discovering the rudder, that Arawana is talking about, in the context of our whole social field.

"To look at art through the optic of life" is what Arawana does by practices that give voice to mother nature (to bridge the ecological divide), to marginalized communities (to bridge the social divide), and to young people and future generations (to bridge the spiritual divide).

Nietzsche's words speak to the essence of Social Presencing Theater because, as Arawana explains, the word "theater" is derived from the Greek *theatron*, a "place for viewing," and from *theasthai* "to behold." So theater is essentially about making something visible. The word "theory" is derived from the Greek *theorein*, which means "to look at." According to some sources, it was used frequently to mean "looking at" a theater stage. In short, theater and theory have a lot more in common than most people might think. Both are essentially about making something visible—which is precisely what Social Presencing Theater does. It makes visible the invisible structures of the social field that shape our collective behavior. Doing this from the optic of an artist means through co-sensing and co-shaping the world. A heightened awareness of our own agency is more necessary now than perhaps ever before in recent history.

So what is Social Presencing Theater? It's a gift. It's a gift that could not have come at a better moment. It's a gift that allows us to better connect to the essence of our humanity and to reshape our relationships from that place. It's a gift that will help us to reimagine and reshape learning and leadership going forward by integrating, science, social art, change, and shifts in awareness from ego to eco, from silo to systems view, by helping us to discover the 'rudder' to navigate our course through the profound challenges of our time.

PROLOGUE

The challenges of our time require bold action based on deep wisdom and care. Each of us has wisdom and boundless capacity to love our natural world and to co-create a good human society. We also need teachings, practices, and each other to do this. We need daily practices that bring forth the clarity and warmth that live in us individually and collectively—activities that nurture our innate creativity. The beauty of daily activities can remind us that everyday living is a creative process. We create meals, family life, emails, food co-ops, teams at work, projects, relationships. Together, with those near us and those around the planet, we co-create the societies in which we live. In this sense, we are all social artists. The question becomes, are we individually and collectively creating the world that we want for our children and their children?

I have spent my life in the performing arts since my first lessons at Miss Gensler's dance studio in Cleveland, Ohio, at the age of five. Meditation practice entered my life nearly fifty years ago. Teaching and co-creating movement experiences in schools, theaters, and community settings has convinced me that social innovation is what people love to do. The interplay of everyday life, meditation, and social change come together in Social Presencing Theater, a set of embodiment activities and reflections that support personal transformation, social creativity, and systems change. Together with colleagues at the Presencing Institute, a global network of individuals and organizations engaged in awareness-based systems change, I have shepherded the creation of this art form since 2004 to bring forth the insight that lives in our embodied intelligence and in the ordinary and yet profound connection that we have with one another.

Social Presencing Theater invites us to tap into our natural creativity and ability to fully embody the "performance" of being human. My intention with this work is to offer movement practices that support people in recognizing their own and others' embodied wisdom, compassion, and courage to act. In the face of today's enormous environmental, social, and spiritual challenges, we can become disconnected from the fundamental human goodness that lives in our embodied presence. I will describe the three streams that have flowed into Social Presencing Theater and shaped my intention—social change, improvisation, and meditative dance. But first I will share a myth from my Japanese heritage about an unorthodox artistic method used in difficult times. Its message is at the heart of this work.

Amaterasu-ōmikami, the goddess of the sun, is the central Shinto deity of Japan. She had two brothers—Tsukiyomi–no-mikoto, the moon, and Susanoo, the storm. Tsukiyomi-no-mikoto was content to share the heavens with his sister. But Susanoo expressed his unhappiness at being relegated to the oceans below by causing havoc that destroyed the balance of Heaven and Earth. He caused extreme weather, desecrated sacred places in nature, and finally killed one of his sister's most beloved attendants.

There was no light or warmth in Heaven or on Earth. Amaterasu-Ōmikami was so angry that she hid herself in a cave. Outside, the community of gods and goddesses gathered. They pleaded and prayed. They brought a rooster, whose crowing would normally signal the first morning light. They brought offerings—a sacred tree on which they hung jewels and a mirror. But the sun did not come out. They became more afraid.

Then the goddess Ame-no-Uzume-no-mikoto stepped forward. She turned over a wooden washtub, stepped up onto the tub, and began a playful dance. She pulled up her skirt and stamped her feet. The community was shocked; as she continued, they began to laugh.

Amaterasu-Ōmikami was curious. Why were they laughing at such a serious time? With curiosity, she rolled back the stone that closed the cave entrance and peeked out. Through the crack she saw her own image of brightness in the mirror that the community had hung in the sasaki tree. Her curiosity and the recognition of her own brilliance seduced her out. The community quickly closed the cave by placing a magical plaited straw rope at its entrance.

It is said that Ame-no-Uzume-no-mikoto is the goddess of arts, entertainment, mirth, revelry, joy, harmony, and meditation. Her praise names mean "the Great Persuader" and "the Heavenly Alarming Female." She is celebrated at the Tsubaki Grand Shrine in Mie, Japan, and her story has been told for generations. She was not overwhelmed by the darkness. She recognized her own role and had the courage (or madness) to act. Her fresh and unexpected gesture celebrated life and was the "true move" that drew the sun from hiding. The community's true move was the wisdom to provide the mirror that allowed the sun goddess to see her own brilliant nature and to return to the world. They did not forget her light.

This story reminds me that today's challenges call for daring and wise action. With Social Presencing Theater we aspire to support the individual and collective true moves that uncover our own personal, organizational, and societal brilliance in order to shine light and warmth on the density of today's challenges.

My story of dance as social change began in the summer of 1968, after the murder of Dr. Martin Luther King Jr. had deepened racial tension and polarization nationally and in traditionally segregated Boston. That summer I began working in a program called Summerthing, a neighborhood arts festival sponsored by the Mayor's Office of Cultural Affairs. In the years that followed I brought together a troupe of young dancers. We created a performance that toured on a mobile stage to all the neighborhoods in Boston that were fractured by violence and mistrust. Half the dancers were Black, half were White, plus myself, an Asian American.

Folks in Black, Irish, Italian, and Southeast Asian neighborhoods and housing projects came out on those hot summer days to watch the performances. Although we were advised that in some neighborhoods we needed to just do our thing and then quickly get out of there, sometimes people hung around and talked with us. Children would ask if we were all in the same family. Summerthing evolved into a dance company called City Dance Theater that brought programs and workshops into Massachusetts schools under the auspices of Young

Figure 1: City Dance Theater, Summerthing, Boston, MA, 1972.
Dancers: Barbara Demps, Arawana Hayashi, Millard Hurley,
Idris Al-Sabry, Jerry Puciato. Photo credit: Janet Hurwitz.

Audience and the kind guidance of its executive director, Jack Langstaff. I remember performing in New York City's Washington Square Park on the first Earth Day, April 22, 1970, joining other artists in environmental activism. Although dancing had played a key role in my personal journey, I then saw how powerfully movement experiences, firmly rooted in communities, schools, and social or environmental issues, fostered embodied learning, collaboration, and healing.

Although my Western dance lineages are ballet and the Merce Cunningham Studio, I am primarily an improviser. I was influenced by the postmodern dancers at Judson Church in the 1960s and 1970s who explored everyday pedestrian movement as dance and expanded the definition of dance itself. One of the most valuable gifts of my dance life has been working with several improvisation performance groups—spontaneously making things up on the spot with others. My life as an improviser began when I met Jamie Cunningham in New York, also in 1968. I remember Jamie once saying right before we went on stage in one of his company's performances, "If you don't feel like doing what we planned, just do whatever you want and I will pick up on it." Never quite knowing what will happen suits me, and it also lives in Social Presencing Theater.

The weight of social and personal chaos of the 1970s and auspicious coincidence brought me to begin studying meditation with Tibetan meditation master and author Chögyam Trungpa, Rinpoche (Rinpoche is a Tibetan title for a revered teacher). He was an artist himself and taught a series of courses on Dharma Art, which he called the activity of nonaggression. He emphasized meditation in action and art in everyday life. He spoke of art as a powerful force in creating what he called enlightened society. His teachings on art can be found in the book

True Perception.[1] He also wrote poems and plays and developed a theater training based on Tibetan monastic dance, which he called Mudra Space Awareness. These teachings are embedded in Social Presencing Theater.

During the few years that I co-directed the dance program at Naropa University in Boulder, Colorado (founded by Chögyam Trungpa), I greatly benefited from a community of colleagues that included dancer Barbara Dilley, actor Lee Worley, poet Allen Ginsberg, musician Jerry Granelli, and many others. The link was firmly established between meditation and art making. Lee, Jerry, and I brought this into the context of education, supporting teachers who wanted to integrate contemplative arts practices into their classrooms in a Rockefeller Foundation–funded Arts in Education Program. Today Social Presencing Theater is a practice field for applying meditative awareness to movement and space.

A suggestion by Trungpa Rinpoche led me to a dance practice that, in appearance, is on the opposite end of the spectrum from improvisation. In 1977, I began studying Bugaku, Japanese court dance, with Suenobu Togi, Sensei (Sensei is a Japanese title for teacher), whose ancestors had been Japanese court musicians and dancers in the Japanese Imperial Household Music Department since the Nara Period, thirteen hundred years ago. The dances have changed very little since then. The complete art form is called Gagaku, elegant music of the Japanese court. Togi Sensei, an accomplished musician as well as a beautiful dancer, eventually joined the faculty of the Ethnomusicology Department of the University of California in Los Angeles. He completely embodied his art form and was an extraordinary teacher. Being his student for thirty years, and performing with friends who also fell in love with this art form, has been one of my life's great blessings.

My experience performing Bugaku confirmed that each moment of the emerging dance was filled with a sense of vastness along with an intimate connection to the other performers and to the audience. Even after performing these dances hundreds of times, each moment felt vivid and direct, uncontrived, and completely ordinary—a moment of living in the body, grounded on the Earth, in the open space of not knowing what comes next. Our troupe of musicians and dancers was of limited accomplishment, and yet the performances created an atmosphere of freshness.

The performance seems like a ritual for brightening the space. It has an effect not unlike ceremonies of smudging (burning sage) or offering juniper smoke—ceremonies that have been performed by indigenous people for thousands of years. These ceremonies clear the atmosphere, enabling positive energy to empower the place and the people. The Bugaku performance seems to evoke energy—perhaps from the open sky to the Earth. At jazz concerts we sometimes hear Black people shout "Ashe" when the music soars. I have heard about Sufis shouting "Allah" at points during the dervish dancing. The art form itself attracts an energy that seems almost like a being.

Bugaku was created hundreds of years ago to bring harmony to the world by joining the vast expanse of vision with the natural and human world. The haunting music, richness of costumes, and the movement patterns of the dancers all create an immediate and timeless beauty. Originally it was only performed in the rarified environment of the Imperial court or at shrines on outdoor stages in natural settings. It is said that the performance attracts *kami*, or gods. It was thought that the art form evoked the peaceful energy of Heaven that leaders needed in order to connect with their inherent wisdom and compassionate leadership. The story reminds me of US Supreme Court Justice Ruth Bader Ginsburg, who listened to opera to feel the fullness of humanity, and I imagine that the art form brought inspiration and strength to her leadership. The idea that the arts can evoke human wisdom and empower enlightened leadership has never left me. It is the DNA of Social Presencing Theater.

Some say that we are now living in a dark age. The global climate crisis, heartbreaking social inequality, structural racism, worldwide health threats, and the solidification of political views that do not allow for dialogue or "stepping into the shoes" of others. All of these conditions contribute to a sense of the darkening of human potential. They are signs of a shutting down of the natural brilliance of human beings. We hold a strong intention that Social Presencing Theater can contribute to uncovering the brilliance of human wisdom—the light of intelligence coupled with the warmth of appreciation, kindness, and care.

The practices are for those of us who celebrate the ordinariness of this moment of life and by doing so perhaps recognize its sacredness. Although Social Presencing Theater is notably different from a brilliant jazz ensemble or serenely spinning dervishes, it too has cultural ancestors—artist-leaders whose performances benefited the world. Being fully present in life's ordinary moments allowed them to connect with a force of wakeful nonstruggle that assisted, guarded, and empowered them as they went about the everyday yet sacred task of creating a good human society. May it be that we, the inheritors, continue to do so as we become the ancestors of those yet to be born.

Over the years, many people have asked for a book about the origins and underlying principles of this work and have offered their support. Two of the early Social

Presencing Theater teachers, Manish Srivastava and Kate Johnson, began collecting what they called nuggets—important themes in the work. These nuggets became a collection of inquiries and principles, which I have done my best to present in this book. There have been many co-creators of Social Presencing Theater, so there are many stories. Mine is just one of them.

For nearly forty years I taught movement classes and created dances. Quite frankly, very few people took an interest. Then, in 2003, I met Otto Scharmer, senior lecturer and action researcher at the Sloan School of Management at Massachusetts Institute of Technology (MIT) in Cambridge, Massachusetts. He is the founding chair of the Presencing Institute. For some reason, he did take an interest. I began working with him and Peter Senge, senior lecturer at MIT's Sloan School and founder of the Society for Organizational Learning, offering awareness and embodiment sessions in their programs. In those days, many participants thought that mindfulness had no place in work life or in a systems change process—and that working with the body on those things was just plain weird. Our morning awareness sessions were sparsely attended. During the embodiment sessions participants often claimed sudden work emergencies or were inexplicably unable to attend.

Otto, Peter, Katrin Kaeufer, and other "respectable" colleagues provided sheltering wings of support. Katrin is executive director of the Presencing Institute and senior research fellow at MIT's Community Innovators Lab (CoLab) in the Department of Urban Studies and Planning. Participants in their programs would say, "Well, if they say it is an important thing to do, we might as well try." Without their support, Social Presencing Theater would not have been able to establish roots in the soil of systems change.

Today, mindfulness is a household word for many people engaged in change work. Many leaders and social innovators recognize the need to cultivate their personal capacities as open-minded thinkers and compassionate listeners. They appreciate the value of stillness and reflection in their lives. In the early years of our collaboration Otto and other colleagues joined the embodiment practices with inquiries into specific social issues, giving birth to Social Presencing Theater. These practices are now an integral part of the methodologies created by the Presencing Institute to support people in organizational and social change efforts.[2]

As a result of this expanded interest, practitioners are developing their own variations and changes in the practices. Some are bringing Social Presencing Theater into the arena of climate and social justice, addressing trauma, conflict, and racial violence. I am pleased to see the proliferation of self-organized, peer-learning Social Presencing Theater gatherings and offerings in Europe, North America, and South America. During the coronavirus pandemic, Social Presencing Theater practitioners developed online courses and gatherings to bring benefit in a world of physical distancing.

As Social Presencing Theater is being taken in multiple directions by multiple practitioners, it seems timely to write down part of its history and share the principles from which it arose. Instructions for some of the practices are included here, but this volume is not intended to be a detailed practice manual. Learning to engage in a movement practice by reading a book has its limitations. In-person and online courses are available. I have included some stories provided by Social Presencing Theater practitioners, and my close colleagues Manish Srivastava and Daniel Ludevig have contributed client case studies. However, the book is primarily about the origins and vision of this work.

Although most people shorten Social Presencing Theater to SPT, I have honored the suggestion of one of my dear readers, Richard Reoch, to use the full name of the work, Social Presencing Theater, throughout the book.

This book was mostly written before the global pandemic and does not include the myriad of Social Presencing Theater online prototypes and offerings. We continue to learn about the power of this work as we engage with one another online. We see the careful attention given by strangers as they witness the embodied shapes of others. We are enriched by the insights shared and inspired by the feeling of global connection. We engage sense perceptions that we did not know we had as we continue to build healthy social fields online. I hope that in the future someone else will write about the evolution of Social Presencing Theater online. I am grateful to those, especially Otto Scharmer and Katrin Kaeufer, who requested (actually, insisted on) this book.

01

INTRODUCING SOCIAL PRESENCING THEATER

Since 2007, I and others have offered Social Presencing Theater programs in Europe, North and South America, Asia, Australia, and Africa. Today, many Social Presencing Theater practitioners are using these methods to bring about change in their organizations and communities. Since 2009, Michael Stubberup, Ninni Sodhal, and others from the Vaekstcenterest meditation community in the tiny village of Norre Snede, Denmark, have hosted yearly gatherings where practitioners and researchers meet to deepen their practice and to integrate awareness meditation with research methods. The hosts cook lunch for us each day, and when we are all gathered, they often introduce us to and describe the dishes they have made. Quite formally, they say the name of each dish. Then they wish us "bon appetit."

Likewise, this book is a somewhat formal introduction to each Social Presencing Theater practice. I begin by introducing Social Presencing Theater as a whole. Many of us have tried, with little success, to develop an "elevator speech" about Social Presencing Theater, but it is not so easy to describe. It lives in a particular professional context that is not familiar to everyone. When I first encountered the world of systems change, I had never heard anyone describe themselves as a change facilitator, and I thought coaching referred to sports. These roles were new to me. Likewise, our use of words like *embodiment, awareness,* and *social field shifts* to describe Social Presencing Theater may not do much to illuminate the work for many people. Over the years, when I have visited my dentist for a check-up, he has sometimes asked me, "And what is it that you do again?" I respond as best I can and watch a cloud of "What is she talking about?" come across his face. It is difficult to come up with a brief description.

Besides asking what it is, one might also wonder why Social Presencing Theater is important. Why would I be interested? Let me return to the Danish lunches. The cooks don't tell us that each dish is nourishing, because we can recognize for ourselves the benefits of the natural ingredients and the care that they have put into the preparations. Likewise, when we engage Social Presencing Theater, we can feel the benefits of the movements and the feelings they generate. But because Social Presencing Theater is a movement art, my ability to capture it in words is very limited. These first two chapters attempt to convey the value of Social Presencing Theater by describing what it is, what some of the underlying principles are, and how it is being used. Throughout the book, brief stories from Social Presencing Theater practitioners highlight the "nutritional value" of the work for yourself and for the "social bodies" with which you work and live.

Meeting the World of Systems Change

Social Presencing Theater was born from auspicious coincidence. In 2001, I joined a team of old friends and colleagues offering creative process sessions at the Shambhala Institute for Authentic Leadership in Halifax, Nova Scotia. The institute hosted remarkable gatherings that attracted many thought leaders and innovators who were interested in the integration of meditation, creative process, and systems change. Peter Senge was one of the original presenters. We on the creative process team had all taught at Naropa University, worked in the field of arts in education, and created performance work together, some of us since the 1970s. We knew little to nothing about organizational development or change management.

Then, in 2003, I was a participant in Otto Scharmer's course at the Shambhala Institute. He was teaching with David Rome, a friend of mine who was presenting the technique called Focusing.[1] I had no idea who Otto was. I was scheduled to teach a forty-five minute creative process session in their module; however, Otto and David had a lot to say, and the time for my part shrank to about ten minutes. The only movement form I knew that could be practiced in ten minutes was Duets (description in chapter six). I needed a partner to help me demonstrate, so I invited Otto to dance with me. I don't think we had any actual verbal conversation at all that week.

In the fall of that same year, Peter invited some of his network to join some of us from the Shambhala Institute for a retreat near Boston. Otto attended. At one point, he unexpectedly turned to me and asked me to join him and Peter at the Society for Organizational Learning's Executive Champions Workshop in Stowe, Vermont. I would offer meditation and "embodied presence" practice. Otto envisioned a capacity-building program that he, Beth Jandernoa, and I would offer the following year.

That was the beginning of the Presencing Foundation Program, which continues to this day. The program offers basic capacity building in applying the change theory Theory U and the practice called *"presencing"*—both articulated by Otto in his writings and teaching. Theory U is a framework and a process that describe stages of change (the U process) that emphasize the qualities of open mind, open heart, and open will of those engaged in organizational and social transformation. During those years I brought the practices called the 20-Minute Dance, The Village, Duets, and Field Dance into capacity-building programs as a way for people to experience the stages of the U process.

Theory U resonated with my own experience of creative process. It described an innovation process that was straightforward and grounded in experience. In 2007, I read about Social Presencing Theater in *Theory U*: "A new social art form I call Social Presencing Theater that stages media events and productions to connect different communities and their transformational stories by blending action research, theater, contemplative practices, intentional silence, generative dialogue, and open space."[2] I wondered what that was.

What Is Social Presencing Theater?

In April 2008, my visionary pal Gregor Barnum and I had a conversation with Otto. We asked, what is Social Presencing Theater? Otto had a vision, and Gregor and I and a team of friends spent a couple of years turning those ideas into community-based performance events. I say more about that later in the book. Today Social Presencing Theater has developed into an individual and group practice rooted in embodiment, meditation, and systems thinking. It engages the body's physical and spatial intelligence—an intelligence that is innate in all of

us but that we don't often attend to. Movement experience elicits genuine insights into our own behaviors and
also into how groups shift from perpetuating stale relationship patterns toward becoming creative entities.
It provokes reflection and learning. It makes visible the
deeper patterns that support the cultivation of healthy
social relations, sparking creative action in teams, organizations, and communities.

Social Presencing Theater got its name from Otto
Scharmer, and the words describe what it is. *Social*
refers to both the *social body*, the physical arrangement
of a group of people in a space, and to the *social field*, the
quality of the relationships between the people. *Presencing*
relates to awareness and a larger sense of environment.
Theater refers to the visible choices we make (what we do)
and the relationships created from those choices (what
we sense). Those choices are determined by our level of
collective awareness, or *social presencing.*

The practice is social because it is engaged in by groups
and teams—social bodies. It invites us into an experience
of social awareness—knowing that is shared by a group.
Individuals engage in a process wherein they are present
and able to collectively "sense into" both their limiting patterns and their wellspring of creative potential.
Individual insights and transformations have great value;
however, many of us realize the need for others as co-creators, partners, supporters, and challengers. We need
others to listen to and hold us, both in our stumblings
and in pursuit of our highest aspirations. There is wisdom
in groups. Often it is hidden under discord and confusion; but it is there. Social Presencing Theater accesses
and makes visible the deeper wisdom that informs our
engagement with complex and demanding issues.

In the book *Theory U*, Otto posits that when we can attend
to the present moment fully, not only do we connect

with a vivid sense of being, but we can also experience a sense of possibility—an emerging future. Collectively we can sense into what has not happened yet, a future in which we have a role to play. He calls this experience *presencing*—a blend of *presence* and *sensing*. When I asked Otto to remind me where the word *presencing* came from, he wrote in a text message, "I saw the word first in the English translation of a Heidegger text by a French translator. I liked it. I was looking for a word like that. Then I googled it. No hits. Nothing came up (it was in the 1990s), except that some nurses talked about presencing when they described their experience with end-of-life care. Then I knew. THAT'S the perfect word that I was looking for. Later I found it in one of my interviews with Henri Bortoft. He didn't use it in the interview, but later, in one of his books he said, 'the whole presences itself within the parts.'"[3]

Presencing is defined as "to sense, tune in, and act from one's highest future potential—the future that depends on us to bring it into being. Presencing... works through 'seeing from our deepest source.'" In other words, we can collectively perceive and experience the present moment without the limitation of our habitual concepts, opinions, or projections. In doing so, we contact our innate intelligence, tender caring, and courage—three qualities that manifest as the true moves we make as we co-create with each other the systems in which we live and work.

The root of the word *theater* comes from the Greek *theatron*—literally, "a place for viewing"—from *theasthal*, meaning "to behold." We use the word theater not in reference to drama or theatrical performance. We use the word in this original meaning—as a place where things become visible. In ancient times and in many cultures, the theater was a place where people enacted ceremonies and rituals for connecting to gods, for healing, for amusement, for good harvests, for mourning, and for making visible the rich stories of what it is to be a human being with other human beings. From times long past until now, theater has been a social form of collective seeing and sensing. People gather to be moved, informed, uplifted, challenged, amused, transformed, and connected. Theater makes visible the fullness of humanity; it is a mirror in which we can see ourselves in all our difficulties and glories in order to experience a transformation and a deeper understanding of what it is to be human.

The practices are called theater not because we are acting or pretending, but because we are embodied physical beings who are visible. Unlike thoughts and words, bodies are visible. We are visible to one another. I am not referring to "body language," the psychological implications of postures and gestures. Instead, our interest lies in movement choices. As we move about with others, we create visible patterns and structures. Because Social Presencing Theater is primarily nonverbal and without goal orientation, it opens our awareness to the subtle ways we communicate through the movement choices we make. Relationships arise and dissolve, creating an ever-changing landscape of possibilities. We make visible the social fields of relationships that we create moment by moment.

Social Presencing Theater consists of a set of nine basic practices, usually engaged in by groups, with variations to adapt to specific contexts and learning arenas: 20-Minute Dance, Dance of Fives, Village, Duets, Field Dance, Stuck, Seed, Case Clinic, and 4-D Mapping. We first did Stuck (chapter three) and 4-D Mapping (chapter four) in 2010 and added "sculptures," physical embodied shapes, to the Case Clinic process soon after. Seed Dance emerged as a practice for linking the crystallizing stage of the U process to the prototyping stage. Case Clinic and Seed Dance are not included in this book; but like Stuck and 4-D Mapping they use a format of moving from an embodied sculpture of the current reality to one that embodies an emerging future. All were created to make visible the shift that happens both in individuals and in social fields.

Each practice has a view, a purpose, and a definite form—how to begin, what the parameters are, when to end. The practices are forms. They are containers for experience. Each practice is followed by a group reflection. There is no right or wrong experience—only learning. The discipline is to welcome all experience as learning. Insights from the practice inform our work or life situation. I would like to emphasize that Social Presencing Theater is a practice that we do regularly to deepen our competence in embodied and spatial knowing. Practice groups meet in many cities; some in person, some online. Practitioners form a supportive peer learning community.

The practices invite a connection or integration of the three bodies—the individual body, the Earth body, and the social body. We cultivate an embodied presence by feeling our individual body grounded and connected to the Earth. This sense of settledness enables our awareness to naturally expand to include the social bodies of which we are a part and the greater sense of environment. We experience our natural connection to others as we engage physically and spatially in a group setting. We act from a sense of the whole, rather than from our individual part and agenda. This integration of the three bodies becomes the ground from which fresh insights and creative actions arise.

The practices require no talent, no previous training. They only require a body, a willingness to trust in "body-knowing," and an openness to fresh possibilities that we do not "think up" or plan. We use simple movements and make physical choices in the space—where to move, when to stop. We make movement choices based on self-awareness, an awareness of the group (the visible arrangement of bodies) and on the felt sense of the experience (the invisible relationship quality).

In addition to becoming aware of ourselves and of others, we are invited to expand or relax our awareness, to summon the open space of possibility. That open space becomes the ground for innovation.

We create spaces where people can move freely and then reflect on what actions or nonactions are needed to create a field of relationships that is wakeful, kind, and creative. The practices invite us to attend carefully to these social fields and to sense the ways they shift from an egocentric focus to ecosystem awareness. In our everyday life and work, the term *egocentric* here simply means that, either individually or collectively, we consider our own interests and well-being without considering the well-being of the global social body and the Earth.

The Ground We Stand On

We hold some grounding principles that establish the integrity of the work. They are the foundation on which Social Presencing Theater was created, and they express a view that is essential if the work is to continue in its truthfulness. They represent an attitude with which to approach the work. They shape not only the form of the practices, but also how we engage in and facilitate the practices with others.

Basic goodness is our innate nature

Social Presencing Theater is based on the premise that basic goodness is the fundamental nature of ourselves, others, and society itself. I am not using the word goodness in a moral sense—good as opposed to bad—but more in the sense of wholeness. I first heard the words *basic goodness* from Tibetan meditation master Chögyam Trungpa, who described it as an innate healthiness and wakefulness inherent in all humanity.[4] There is a lot of evidence that this might not be true. Terrible, terrible things happen every day to people, to animals, to the natural world. However, the teachings on basic goodness invite us to see and sense what is underneath fear, aggression, and stupidity. Social Presencing Theater invites us to contact the unconditional wholesomeness that lives in us all.

Basic goodness is a view or an attitude that sees an underlying sanity in everyone and in systems. An opposite view would be to believe that individuals, including oneself, are basically "messed up," or that organizations of individuals are toxic to the core. The view of fundamental healthiness is not ignorant of neurosis and dysfunction. It is not blind to the fact that people treat each other badly. However, having positive regard for others prevents us from buying into a narrative that people and systems are at their core corrupt and unworkable. It invites us to turn toward our and others' shadows and "stuck" places with clarity of mind and gentleness of spirit. It tempers a tendency to think that it is our job to fix, change, or save everyone around us. It loosens the habit of thinking that we know better, that we occupy the higher moral ground, that we have the solution to other people's problems. In Social Presencing Theater we begin by acknowledging that wisdom lives in all systems, individual and collective, and that change is a naturally unfolding process. We have the privilege of accompanying, out of genuine care, the journey of our fellow humans as we collectively discover our way forward.

Awareness opens and transforms experience

The mind has a fantastic ability to simply notice. The practices invite us to notice the moment-by-moment unfolding of experience. Noticing experience is, of course, not the same as thinking about experience. Awareness is a direct knowing, a felt noticing. Awareness is knowing where we are, what we are doing, how we feel, and what we think. It is also knowing presence and the social atmosphere in which we live. Awareness is always available. However, when our mind is occupied with memories, opinions, assumptions, and imaginings, open awareness can be obscured. When thoughts about what we want or don't want occupy all of our mind space, we lose touch both with our sensing body and with the felt awareness.

Given today's speed and pressures and the amount of time we spend in front of our computer screens and devices, many of us notice a disconnect and imbalance between our thinking mind, feeling heart, and active body. We can feel pulled in multiple and opposite directions. Without taking deliberate time to settle into a sense of wholeness, we can live in a mental world of projections. With hindsight, I notice that frequently I do not actually sense "in" to my body or sense "out" into the environment with much accuracy. I am often not settled enough to really listen to what a colleague is saying, let alone feel the full resonance of what is said. I am on to the next online meeting, throwing what was said into some category or opinion in my mind without really considering or feeling it. I wonder, where was my awareness?

A workshop attendee told me that he had recently received professional feedback that he had become a "talking head." He resonated with the expression, "My body is just a transportation system that carries my brain from meeting to meeting." He became aware of a disconnect between his body, his mind, and the environment. His awareness noticed physical and mental stress. It noticed that people were not actually listening to him; that he was less effective than he knew he could be. He noticed a growing distance from family members. His innate intelligence told him that things were out of balance. The awareness that noticed this disconnect was not in itself disconnected.

Awareness is the leverage point for change. When we suddenly become aware that we are lost in thought and disconnected from our body and the environment, that noticing immediately shifts us into a moment of connection. We experience being fully present, even if just for a second. My colleague Antoinette says that gardening, feeling her body engaged with the activity of planting and weeding, is her therapy. Some of us feel our body and mind naturally synchronize when we are doing yoga, walking in the woods, or sitting on the porch doing nothing. When our mind is less active and our feeling body is more grounded, we appreciate that awareness is naturally present. Most of us yearn to experience this more regularly or consistently, even in the midst of the speed, uncertainty, and demands of life.

The intensity of the world situation, work, and daily pressures can cause us to contract. We try to hold all the pieces together, try to get control of our schedules, multiple projects, kids, work teams, eating habits, finances. We try to do the right thing, be available, keep all the balls in the air, manage. But maybe trying harder, focusing more, and doubling down are not the answer. My meditation teacher, Trungpa Rinpoche says in the book *True Perception*, "In the case of awareness experience, there is simply appreciation. Nothing is hassling us or demanding anything from us. Instead by means of awareness practice, we could simply tune in to the phenomenal world both inwardly and outwardly.[5]

Open mind, open heart, and open will are essential leadership qualities in these challenging times[6]

Presencing work is grounded in the recognition that all beings can cultivate a mind of curiosity and sanity, a heart of wisdom and compassion, and a will of courage and strength.[7] These inherent human qualities can be deepened and strengthened. We can actually practice being more open-minded and open-hearted when habit inclines us to enclose ourselves in narrow behaviors and ideas. "Presencing work" assumes that human beings care about one another and do not want to destroy the planet and themselves. It recognizes the "three divides" that challenge our times—the disconnects we experience from the natural world, from each other, and from our own true nature.

However, we can think, speak, and act from our deepest resources of kindness and creativity. We can engage in work and life from a place of appreciation and also hold a sadness of heart when we experience the "absencing" that we and others engage in. Absencing refers to the ways in which we fail to acknowledge our own basic goodness.[8] Social Presencing Theater practices reveal our blind spots and also our natural insightfulness. They are an invitation to touch our collective tenderheartedness and the clarity, kindness, and bravery that we need to create a good society today.

Creativity arises from nowness

Nowness is a word used by Chögyam Trungpa to describe the true nature of our experience—that every moment is open, spacious, and vividly present. I remember once hearing him say that nowness is a state without struggle. We do not deny the depth of suffering and trauma that we individually and collectively carry from the past into the present. We are not bypassing the complexity or power that the past holds. Social Presencing Theater practices invite us to experience whatever we experience, without denial, and also to suspend and let go of our thoughts and conceptual interpretation about that experience. We let those go in order to stay with the rawness of the feeling and allow the present moment to be as it is. True creativity arises from the very moment of nowness. It does not depend on our cleverness. Nor does it depend on our training (although engaging in discipline is, of course, important). Nowness enables us to face forward and take the next step in our work of creating a good society.

Making a true move is powerful engagement

Basic goodness, awareness, openness, nowness—all well and good—but how do these qualities show up in everyday life? These are intangible values, and we live in a difficult and pragmatic world that needs skillful action. I refer earlier in the book to the true move. The true move is the enactment of these non-material qualities. Social Presencing Theater, like many art practices, joins intangible qualities with materiality. The inseparability of the invisible and the visible lives in each moment. When the limited, self-conscious self is not thinking and planning, our movements and words arise naturally as the true move.

False moves in gesture or speech express a disconnect between the thinking mind, the genuine heart, and the engaged body. They lack resonance with their exterior surroundings. They are an expression of speed or anxiety. The true move is fresh. It is powerful in its directness and simplicity. It cuts through staleness and confusion. Social Presencing Theater is the practice of making true moves, and it is, indeed, a practice—something we *do* over and over again. It is not something we try once, put in our arsenal of trendy change methodologies, and turn to when we need something a little different. By practicing we begin to discern when the true move appears and what the conditions for its appearance are. When we engage with subtlety, we begin to notice spontaneous genuineness. We gain confidence in the true move as the full expression of this moment of life.

When I first met the world of systems change, I called my work The Art of Making a True Move. It was a series of improvisation and performance practices that were expressions of meditation in action or art in everyday life. If I remember correctly, the title came from looking at a book of photographs of the Russian ballet dancer Vaslav Nijinsky, who danced in the early twentieth century. The photos captured images of him dancing. A friend looking at the photos with me remarked that there were no images in which Nijinsky was making a false move. To me, this meant that his body and mind were completely engaged, unselfconscious, and present in every photo. I reflected on this idea of a true move. Can I access the one genuine gesture of this present moment?

Appreciating daily details is art in everyday life

I love this observation by Trungpa Rinpoche: "Everyday life is a work of art if you see it from a point of view of nonaggression."[9] The Social Presencing Theater practices do not force or manipulate experience. They invite us to appreciate what is. This is an expression of nonaggression that can inform our everyday life. We engage genuinely in the moment-to-moment unfolding of our movements. This habit continuously draws our attention to the present moment and begins to permeate our ordinary, everyday lives—how we carry ourselves, how we regard challenges, how we relate with others. We appreciate the tasks and conversations that constitute our daily routines. Our gestures and words arise from awareness. These true moves, full of presence and appreciation, express the unique moments of our daily lives.

In every moment we co-create our experiences and the social bodies that we inhabit. We face challenges, conflicts, and uncertainty daily. The core concepts and practices of Social Presencing Theater provide a foundation for engaging creatively with the vicissitudes of life. They help us align with our deeper values and commitments in order to create what is most important. We can strengthen and celebrate our collective will to enact the true moves that will bring benefit to our world.

A Simple Everyday Life Practice

Here is a simple everyday life practice.

Go to the window. Sit or stand there for five minutes and look out. Don't do anything. Don't try. Just sit there and look out. Thoughts will come and go. Let them. Don't try to relax. Just sit there. Without any special effort, awareness is there. Awareness tells us what we see and how we feel. Awareness is always present.

Then take up a journal or piece of paper. Write down one short phrase or sentence describing something you saw or heard while looking out the window. Just describe it in a few words without interpretation. Next, write a short phrase that describes a feeling you had as you looked out the window. Finally, write a short phrase that joins your perception with your feeling. Write down your first thought without laboring over it. Then read the three lines back to yourself and notice how you feel.

02

USES AND BENEFITS OF SOCIAL PRESENCING THEATER

Social Presencing Theater is used by an ever-growing network of people in multiple sectors and locations as they apply Theory U in their personal, organizational, and larger ecosystem change work. This theory of change grows out of decades of work done at the Massachusetts Institute of Technology (MIT) in systems thinking, organizational learning, and action research.[1] It is a framework that emphasizes the vital importance of the "interior condition," the state of mind and heart of leaders bringing change to their organizations and communities.[2] It posits that in this time of severe disruption we cannot simply rely on what we have learned from the past. We can gain capacity from *presencing*, attending to, and learn from an emerging future.

Theory U is also a set of principles, practices (including Social Presencing Theater), and change processes that cultivate the curious mind, compassionate heart, and courageous will in order to help change-makers engage collectively in actions that create social fields of well-being for all on the planet. The theory is being applied in large multi-sector systems change projects. For the purposes of this book, however, the descriptions of the U process pertain to a journey by individuals and teams within the framework of Social Presencing Theater. This journey does not simply apply what we already know to the challenges we face. It innovates and manifests in three stages: first, seeing and sensing deeply into the context; then, allowing stillness and fresh insights to emerge; and finally, engaging in a process of prototyping the new.

Besides being a framework and a set of methodologies, Theory U offers a new narrative and language for co-creating positive change. At a time in which our systems are collapsing and breaking down, a time of crises affecting the environment, health care, social issues, government, finance, farming, and education, Theory U offers an invitation and guide for engagement. Social Presencing Theater contributes to the application of the U process by joining the physical and spatial intelligence with emotional and cognitive intelligence.

The magic in these practices happens when we stop thinking, planning, and manipulating and instead begin to trust our body-knowing and a sense of open space. Then we individually and collectively can tap into the natural wisdom and creativity that are often hidden underneath all our learned and habitual opinions, judgments, and fears. Social Presencing Theater offers the adventure of engaging physically with others to enact, or make visible, what words and thoughts are not able to express.

The practices are being used by facilitators, coaches, and leaders for personal development, for cultivating high-performance teams, for creating new products or processes, for moving from "stuck" situations to creative flow, and to develop collective awareness of both organizational and social systems. They invite deep reflection and brave action. They engage the whole person—body, mind, and heart. They work quickly—they get to the point. They engage people's natural creativity and deep care for one another. Social Presencing Theater appeals to our true human nature to work together to bring something beneficial into the world. It is for people looking for insights into both how change happens and how they can best shepherd new approaches and initiatives. Let's look briefly at several ways that Social Presencing Theater is being applied.

As a change intervention—disrupting business as usual

In 2008, Otto, Beth Jandernoa, and I brought a version of 4-D Mapping (described in chapter five) to the women's clothing company Eileen Fisher, Inc. Using this method, the company members made a physical map of the company by placing themselves in relation to each other. The map enabled those who were gathered to sense more deeply into the relationships among the founder, the creative designers, the other departments in the company, the stores, and the customers. Everyone present from the company co-created an embodied map of where they experienced their place in the company and their relationships with each other and with customers.

The practice enabled them to slow down and tune into their bodies and their context to gain a deeper understanding of the current situation of their organization. Once they were arranged in the map they could see and sense themselves as a system. From this map, which we call a "social sculpture," they moved carefully to place themselves in a second sculpture that embodied a possible future for the company. Their movements revealed how each person's choice could be meaningful in the co-creation of the future. The social sculpture became a mirror that sharply revealed the company's challenges and aspirations, leadership and team dynamics, and insights about customer relations that influenced the transformation that the company was undertaking at that time. From this, a direction for action arose more quickly than if the company members had only been talking about their future.

Since the early 2000s, Social Presencing Theater has brought clarity and innovation in a myriad of contexts—to banks in Europe and South Africa, to doctors in Ohio, to government leaders in Indonesia, to high school students and teachers in South Central Los Angeles, to corporations in France, to midwives in Uruguay, and to rural women in India. It has been used by city governments in Italy and by the United Nations Country Team in Cambodia. In spite of the newness and unconventionality of the method, it has found its way into social projects and organizations both large and small. The practices are created for teams and organizations with a desire to bring about change and an appetite for a fresh approach. Creating and reflecting on embodied social sculptures reveals deep structural patterns of behavior and thought.

To support leadership development

When leaders feel grounded in their own embodied presence, they are able to tune into their surroundings, to listen with equanimity, to speak with clarity. They lead with a larger perspective. Leaders express that through engaging in the practices they have become better observers, and they find they are more comfortable with uncertainty. Many have shared that the simple practice of the Field Dance (chapter ten) remains an important experience in their leadership development. They learned to trust situations more easily. They gained confidence that they did not need to strain to impress others, but could rest in a sense of authentic presence.

Ivette Guillermo-McGahee is founder and executive director of Allies in Caring, an organization that provides community health and well-being services in New Jersey. She is not only a leader in her organization, but also a civic leader who speaks on behalf of Mexican Americans and others in the Latinx community. She told me that Social Presencing Theater practices and reflections had improved her ability to communicate with her board, made her feel less competitive, and made her more confident that there is "space for everyone to shine."

As a teaching tool

Social Presencing Theater is primarily applied in social or organizational change efforts, but for those of us who teach, the practices bring concepts easily into experience. For instance, a Swiss business school professor told me that the Field Dance, in which a standing person spontaneously performs a gesture that arises from an awareness of a social context, provided students with a direct and vivid participation in a social field, as well as a sense of "letting go" and "letting come," two gestures in a U process.

I frequently use the Duet practice (chapter six) when teaching the four types of listening: 1. listening to confirm what we already know or think; 2. listening for facts and disconfirming data; 3. listening from empathy; and 4. generative listening.[3] Experiencing generative listening through the body in nonverbal practice is quite different from grasping the concept in the mind alone.

As a performance art

In 2008, a small team began to create short inter-view-based performance events to spark community conversations. Over the years the work moved away from performance to small team engagement. Then, in 2019 a few colleagues gathered to again explore its origins as a performance art. In two Social Arts Studio Residencies held in Mexico, they created and performed short theater events to bring visibility to the richness of the local Mayan community. The result, Social Field Resonance practice, a contemplative reflection on visual art and performance, has become a method for enabling audience participants to sense themselves not solely as individuals, but as a social system.

Figure 2: Performance at Hacienda Ochil, Mexico, 2019. Performers: Daniela Ferraz, Kobun Kaluza, Penelope Phylactopoulos, Ninni Sodahl, Miguel Labas, Ricardo Dutra, Arawana Hayashi. Photo credit: Janson Cheng.

Figure 3: Research gathering at Norre Snede, Denmark, 2019.
Photo credit: Ricardo Dutra.

In action research methodology

Ricardo Dutra heads a small research team that currently explores three questions: Are there archetypal ways that leaders, teams, and organizations get stuck? What are the conditions that enable them to move forward in fresh and creative ways? Can we create a pattern language around field shifts from stuckness to innovation? Engaging the body's intelligence is part of the action research methodology. The research team collects data by: paying close attention to their experience of field shifts while personally engaged in the practices; observing and looking for patterns as others engage in the practices; recording and analyzing experiences using photos, drawings, and videos; conducting interviews; and creating tools. These awareness-based methods increase their understanding of the subtle shifts in social fields that can make a significant impact on teams and organizations.

In online courses and gatherings

In 2020, shortly after the beginning of the global coronavirus pandemic (Covid-19), the Presencing Institute launched two online initiatives: GAIA (which attracted 13,000+ participants) and the U.Academy. Social Presencing Theater practices featured prominently in both. Since 2015, the Theory U framework and practices have been shared widely via a massive open online course (MOOC) called u.lab: Leading from the Emerging Future.[4] At this writing in 2020, over 160,000 people from 185 countries have been introduced to Theory U, presencing, and Social Presencing Theater via u.lab.

Many Social Presencing Theater practitioners have offered online opportunities for practice and are prototyping new virtual forms. I must admit I was wary of online Social Presencing Theater. However, experience is dissolving that skepticism. After sharing my embodied physical shape in an online breakout group, I received insightful reflections from two complete strangers in different parts of the world. Somehow through this virtual medium, the essence of my expression had been clearly seen. Their reflections brought clarity to my inquiry.

How One Organization Used Social Presencing Theater

Most practitioners report that they use Social Presencing Theater because it gets to the essential social patterns deeply and quickly. Part of the power of the practice is that it is unfamiliar; people cannot fall back on their usual ways of approaching issues. A friend asked me to help design an intervention that he could use in a social nongovernmental organization (NGO). One issue troubling the organization was a fractured leadership team. Members shared an underlying vision, but views on how to move forward diverged greatly. Some team members were aligned with the team leader, and some were not. Most of the conversations about this problem were held outside of meetings, although the team had tried to talk about it several times, with no traction. Some team members were aware that they were pushing their individual agendas, but they also were certain that their way was best. Some voices were dismissed and labeled as "on some other wavelength." Talking about the issue was leading nowhere. My friend asked whether we could try a Social Presencing Theater practice. We designed the following step-by-step process for this particular organization.

Step One: We framed the experience as an innovative method with a track record for helping teams break through impasses.

We did not try to "sell" the practice or its benefits. We decided to not even use the name Social Presencing Theater, since this team was only vaguely familiar with Theory U. We found that humor worked well when approaching this group. Of course, trust between the facilitator and the team created rapport. My friend's personal embodied presence, plus his confidence that the practice would be helpful, were the keys to opening others' willingness to engage.

Step Two: We communicated the purpose of the practice and why we thought it would be helpful.

We explained that the practice was designed to highlight the shared experience of being paralyzed as a group, unable to navigate in a time of uncertainty. We acknowledged the individual opinions and emotions of the team members when talking about their differences but explained that the practice would invite them to notice if there was a deeper level of shared feeling. They needed a change in perspective—something to shake them out of their usual way of approaching issues. A holistic, embodied approach would shed light on how team members with diverse views could find some common ground to move ahead as a whole, rather than remain stuck as warring parts. In this case, a simple variation on a practice we call Stuck (described in chapter three) seemed like an accessible approach. One team member said, "We've tried everything else, so might as well try this."

Step Three: We gave instructions succinctly and with precision.

Simple, clear instructions allowed people to step into an unfamiliar experience. They gave participants something to hold on to. Clear instructions created a learning container, or holding space, in which the team could relax as they engaged in something that seemed risky. We spoke the instructions, wrote them on a flip chart, and physically demonstrated the practice. Demonstrating opened a space of vulnerability. The instructions defined what kind of movements to use (simple, ordinary movements) and how to pay attention (attend to the experience of the body and the sense of the whole space).

Step Four: The team engaged in the practice.

The team created a group sculpture embodying their current situation. By choosing a level (sitting or standing), a distance between each other, and a direction to face, they created a group sculpture. Then without planning, but by feeling the body and attending to the whole social setup, they sensed where the team body wanted to move. The whole process took only a few minutes.

Step Five: They reflected on the process.

What did they notice? What choices had they made? The group described some of the moments or events that they remembered. "I noticed that some of us just sat on the side and did not want to interact." "I was surprised at how difficult it was to feel connected to others." And "I tried to get everyone to stick together." These were simple observations and descriptions that opened the shared space for a conversation. Rather than arguing, their conversation arose from a reflective space of careful listening. Something had shifted in the way they were relating to one another.

The team members could feel themselves as a collective. They shared their frustration and sadness about their current situation. Some team members were surprised that they felt empathy for the team leader, recognizing the pressure he was under. One insight was that it was not helpful to "check out" and let others on the team solve their dilemma. In the second sculpture, two team members with opposing views ended up standing side by side, both looking in the same direction. This opened up a conversation about a possible collaboration between two differing parties. Embodying their sense of being stuck, and moving with one another, stimulated a kind of intelligence and creativity that they had not been able to access by only thinking and talking.

Step Six: They applied what they learned in the practice to their particular situation.

By being loyal to their direct experience, the group uncovered fresh insights and next steps. By dropping story lines from the past and assumptions about the future, everyone on the team recognized that they needed each other to find a new way of working together. This could have been easily said, but when it was an embodied, felt experience it resulted in action. The practice brought lightness and flexibility into the group. The team members felt more rapport with one another and decided to make a "fresh start." The conversation after the practice was slower and more spacious—no talking over one another. Members were more open to listening to others' views without solidifying immediately around differences. They were able to name the power dynamics in the group, which was a turning point in their conversation and brought a sense of relief. Two team members with opposing views volunteered to head a project together around something they both valued. The team gained confidence that they had a group intelligence that could resolve their issue.

This chapter provides an overview of the ways in which Social Presencing Theater is being used in the world today, creating visibility for our embodied knowledge. The body and its movements in space are a language. Some of us are "native speakers" of this language. Others are learning how to observe and communicate with this nonverbal vocabulary. We gain confidence to feel into each moment and then to step forward from there to innovate a future. We recognize the details and are aware of the social fields that we inhabit and co-create. We know because we directly experience and feel them. The practices I've described increase sensitivity to how each of us creates the social reality moment by moment through the choices we make. Through these practices we orient ourselves from a place of coherence between our own embodiment and the social systems in which we live.

03

FROM THE PRESENT TO THE EMERGING FUTURE: STUCK

Let's turn now to the practices themselves. In this chapter we look at Stuck, the process that transforms a present challenge into a future possibility. It is a method for letting go of a pattern or habit that blocks natural creativity in order to move toward possibilities we aren't yet even aware of. Letting go of personal habitual patterns, no matter how inappropriate or useless they are, is often not easy. The difficulty is only magnified by the cultural patterns of teams, organizations, and the larger systems we are a part of. Intellectually, we can recognize patterns of thought, speech, and action that are hurtful to ourselves and others. Often they go against our highest aspirations and values. Yet even when we acknowledge them, they often persist.

The practice called Stuck has had a transforming effect on individuals and teams over the past decade. It is not an intellectual analysis or a psychotherapeutic approach. It is rooted in the body's natural creative expression, in its longing to move freely. The Stuck practice involves making a small gesture while following the U journey. That gesture imprints on the body in a way that holds the potential for big impact. Insight gained from the gesture can shift how a person thinks about their situation, how they feel about it, and what action they might take. It expresses the power in what Michael Stubberup, a colleague in Denmark, calls "the smallest possible change."[1] Michael says that a small shift goes unnoticed by the forces in ourselves and in our social systems that resist and fight against change. Small changes sneak into our system without causing pushback.

In the Stuck practice, we begin by creating what we call Sculpture 1, an embodied form of an aspect of current reality that is not moving forward, not thriving. Nearly everyone has current relationships, projects, or aspirations that have gotten stuck or bogged down, or that feel thorny. We reflect on a particular situation in our work or life and then make a physical shape that reflects that experience. Sculpture 1 could present itself as a question, a challenge, or a problem. It could be something that is dying or that has outlived its usefulness. It could be an outer obstacle, such as an unsupportive boss or inadequate funding. Or it could be an inner obstacle, such as a lack of confidence or direction. The Stuck practice works for any type of challenge.

We engage with the felt sense of the constraining forces, internal or external, rather than with the emotional reactions that those constraints elicit. In the Stuck practice, identifying what is hindering our movement clarifies the situation. These forces may be concretely in mind or only vaguely sensed. For instance, you might feel you are being pushed down or held down. You might feel you are being

Figure 4: Stuck Practice, Norre Snede, Denmark, 2019. Els Laenens.
Photo credit: Ricardo Dutra.

pulled in different directions, or, in spite of your vision, you might feel held back. You might feel twisted, with your eyes focused to the right and your feet pointed to the left. Stuck is not about acting, pretending, or miming. It is not psychodrama. (I am certain that psychodrama has merit; I am simply clarifying that it is not part of this practice.) Stuck practice is an invitation to physicalize an aspect of your current situation in which forces feel constraining.

We have probably approached this nonmoving situation in our usual ways—thinking about it, talking about it, trying to make others change, trying to change ourselves. However, even if our Stuck is brutally uncomfortable, even if we want it to change, its familiarity has power. It is our Stuck. And both staying with that sensation and letting go of it can be unsettling. The Stuck practice asks us to stay with the feeling but to let go of our past stories about the situation—what we know—so that we might move toward what we do not know, embodied in a second body shape, Sculpture 2. We open ourselves to a future that wants to emerge through us. The process asks us to trust that insight will come from the body and the social body without planning or manipulating.

That requires curiosity and confidence in ourselves and in others. By suspending judgments, we experience our and others' tender hearts. Social Presencing Theater practitioners have learned that staying with the discomfort of the stuck shape until it wants to move, feeling the support and care of others, and engaging in group reflection has profound effects on both work and personal challenges.

The journey from Sculpture 1 to Sculpture 2 is a small transformation based on the U process and social field awareness. We sense into the body experience, let go of any preformed goal, and let uncontrived movement come. When I drop my ideas about who did what to whom to create this stuck situation, then I can attend fully to where my body wants to move. I trust that my body and the social body supporting me actually have some knowledge as we move into the second shape. I give up trying to fix or change the situation and simply open to a sense of possibility. As I become aware of and begin to operate from the social whole, I sense the potential that lives in the social field of connection. Nobody gets stuck without "help" from others. We are all tangled in webs of forces that contribute to our personal and societal stuck situations. By embodying those forces, by deeply sensing into them, I begin to know how the whole system needs to shift in order for me, as an individual, to be free to move.

We enter Sculpture 1 as separate parts—a stuck person and three or four others who embody the forces preventing that person from moving. Each person experiences their individual body and place in the sculpture. By resting attention on the feeling of the individual body and the sculptural shape that the bodies together create, the quality of the relationships between individuals becomes vivid. This invisible, yet experienced quality of relationships is the social field—the interior, felt quality of this social body.

As participants let go of thoughts, plans, and the sense of separate "me-ness," and let go of their particular relationship to the stuck person, they enter an open space of not knowing. They open their attention to the entire social sculpture, which begins to move without knowing where it is going. I often have the sensation that my team and I are in a small boat leaving the familiar shore and floating out into the vast ocean.

Social field awareness is the only paddle or rudder available to the small boat (the social body) as it moves out from Sculpture 1 into the unknown. The shift in attention from the small sense of me to the larger sense

Figure 5: Stuck practice, Presencing Institute Masterclass, Cambridge, MA, 2010. Photo credit: Kelvy Bird.

of the social field and the open space of not-knowing ini-tiates the movement from Sculpture 1 to Sculpture 2. I let go of what I expect to happen or what I think would be best. I let go of trying to control or manipulate the expe-rience. I let go of trying to fix or help the stuck person. I let go of thinking I know the right solution or what a good outcome would be. My attention shifts, from "What am I going to do here? What do I want to happen?" to "Where does the entire organism, the social body system, want to move?"

Because nobody knows where or how the sculpture will move, everyone pays careful attention. This is the practice of letting come, allowing whatever will happen to happen. The movements during the few minutes' journey from Sculpture 1 to 2 unfold naturally because no one person is directing the movement or imposing their will on the others. From this awareness of the social field and the open space of possibility, the group is presencing its Sculpture 2. Continuing the boat metaphor, at some point the group begins to sense that they are headed somewhere. They sense a new place. They are headed toward Sculpture 2. The social body moves as it wants to. The parts shift, find new places, create new relationships as Sculpture 2. This process sets the stage for reflection and dialogue.

By intensifying and staying with that stuck shape, we contact the yearning embodied in the shape to move toward a next step. Stuck wants to move. However, this is not a problem-solution method. Sculpture 2 is not "unstuck," as in a solution to a problem. Sculpture 2 offers a sense of what a next step might be in the journey. It can reveal an insight, a message, a knowing that we do not even know we have. It is not a solution. It points us in a direction. It guides and empowers our next move—the true move.

The first prototype of the Stuck practice was in 2009, while I was experimenting with the presencing methodology called the Case Clinic.[2] I was using this peer coaching process to create a Social Presencing Theater performance. After the case giver described a case, the group created images and small scenes that reflected aspects of the case. When we put these together, they created tiny rituals that expressed the essential aspects of the case. This opened a connection between Social Presencing Theater and ritual— not in the sense of repeating something from the past, but more as a way of connecting with patterns that were prevalent beyond just one case. These enactments of the case opened a deeper understanding of both the blocking and the releasing elements.

In the fall of 2010, I proposed a version of this for a session of the Presencing Masterclass, a two-year program for eighty global leaders in the application of Theory U in multi-stakeholder change initiatives. After I had made my proposal to our small faculty group of five, Otto suggested using the theme of "stuck," embodying a feeling that was restricted and letting a shift happen. So we tried this out in two steps: first, one of us embodied a stuck shape and asked others to make a group sculpture by embodying the restricting forces. After the five people formed the sculpture, they put their full attention on their embodied experience, sensing where the collective sculpture wanted to move. They followed that movement to its conclusion and then engaged in dialogue about their experience. The following day we introduced it to the Masterclass participants, and that was the birth of Stuck.

Practice and Reflection Instructions

Step One: Sit in a small group. One by one, show your embodied stuck shape (Sculpture 1) to the others. After everyone has demonstrated their shape, reflect briefly by simply sharing what you saw or felt as you witnessed each person, without any judgment or interpretation of the gesture. Always speak from the "I" voice about your own experience; never project what you think the stuck person is experiencing.

Step Two: Beginning with the first person, again show your Sculpture 1 stuck shape. Feel your embodied shape and remain there until the body begins to move. Move from Sculpture 1 to Sculpture 2. Move without thinking or planning. When the movement stops[3], say one word or a phrase that arises from the sculpture. If the sculpture itself had a voice, what would it say? The others in the group briefly share their experience as witnesses, saying only "I saw" or "I felt." Next, the second person goes through the same process. Continue until everyone has completed this part of the practice. Take care to keep reflections brief and related directly to the experience. Speak only about your own experience.

Step Three: First person, build a group sculpture around your personal stuck shape. Ask others to embody forces that are restricting movement. Invite and direct the others verbally (do not place them) one by one to a position and shape that intensifies the feeling of the forces in play. Do not tell others what movements to make or how they should feel.

Step Four: After remaining for a minute in the stuck social body sculpture and fully experiencing it, move as a group from Sculpture 1 to Sculpture 2. Move with an awareness of yourselves as a social body. Give up any ideas about helping or fixing and allow the body and the space to guide the shift to Sculpture 2.

Step Five: Without thinking or planning, each person speaks a sentence from their shape and place in the social sculpture. The person bringing the Stuck is the last person to speak. Then all group members share details about their experience, using "I saw" or "I felt" (the "I" voice), and engage in open conversation about the shared experience.

The Philosophy of Stuck

Often I teach with my colleague Manish Srivastava, who is a brilliant consultant, social activist, and poet. He has been on the faculty of several of our year-long advanced Social Presencing Theater trainings in both the US and in Germany. In one of these advanced trainings he presented what he named "the philosophy of stuck" based on our previous teachings. This philosophy helped us clarify some of the guiding principles that are at the heart of the practice, holding both its intention and its integrity:

Stuck is not a problem

Obstacles appear when we are creating something new. Gregor Barnum, former director of corporate consciousness at Seventh Generation, Inc., talked about the Stuck as a big "no." He said, "NO is a design element. Restraint is necessary to get to the lift." Obstacles are a natural part of any creative change process. I often think that "flow" is highly overrated. Stuck is so interesting and juicy. It is the opposite of moving, the opposite of freedom. It is uncomfortable in one way or another. We can become paralyzed by over-contracting inward. We can be too focused on our inner situation, whether that is personal or institutional, ignoring outside forces and the larger context. We can be overextended, distracted, pulled or scattered in different directions, without clear boundaries or priorities. It is difficult not to think of these situations as problems. Often we are stymied by a disconnect between what our head thinks, our heart feels, and our body does.

Through our practice, we suspend the habit of labeling this nonflowing situation as a problem. We don't try to get rid of our sticky situation prematurely. Instead, we welcome it. We turn toward it and say, "Wow, this is terrific! I have a Stuck! You are welcome here." Instead of feeling guilty or ashamed, we are pleased to become fully

FROM
SCULPTURE
ONE
TO
SCULPTURE
TWO

Figure 6: Stuck practice, Eileen Fisher Learning Lab, New York, 2017.
Edinson R. Castano. Photo credit: Ricardo Dutra.

acquainted with our challenge and to really listen to what it has to say. You don't want to outsource your issue to a professional problem solver. Your Stuck is full of wisdom. Lean toward it, feel it. Listen.

Stuck is not you

The situation is temporary. You are full of wisdom and creativity. We often say, "I am stuck." But in this case we say, "I *have* a Stuck" or "I have been the caretaker of an immovable situation for some time now." Maybe it is a fresh obstacle that has recently appeared. Or maybe it is a mature, seemingly intractable situation—one you have been wrestling with for some time. Either way, it is perfect for our practice here. It is not solid. It is not you.

> If you are going to draw a picture, you have to have space in which to paint the picture, which is the canvas or the paper. Similarly, there is a basic space in which confusion occurs. Once there is an explosion of confusion, then there is a gap as well, which is anti-explosion or anti-confusion. The positive and the negative are both part of the situation, we could say. So there is always room, a gap, in which inspiration and discipline can function.[4]
>
> —Chögyam Trungpa

Figure 7: Stuck practice, Eileen Fisher Learning Lab, New York, 2017.
Lynda Sing. Photo credit: Ricardo Dutra.

Nobody is stuck by themselves

External and internal forces can seem to prevent us from accomplishing our intention—an interconnected, often hidden, web of causes and conditions. We are part of families, teams, organizations, communities, and larger social systems, as well as ecological, economic, political, educational, and health care systems. Any of these can hold us back, push us down, or block our journey. And of course, sometimes our own body, heart, and mind seem to get in the way, blocking us from connecting with our potential. Our own hesitation or feelings of defeated-before-we-begin hold us back.

By sharing our embodied stuck shapes, we reveal the truth that we all have places in our lives that are not moving forward. Since there are always multiple causes and conditions holding us back or stretching us in different directions (for instance, between work and family), we need a method that allows us to feel the richness of our situation and also shows us a direction and a place to put our next step.

Stuck is the perfect invitation for learning

You and your Stuck are the perfect pair. You want to learn; Stuck is the perfect teacher. When we regard our life circumstances as either good or bad, success or failure, win or lose, we are not in a learning mode. When we regard our situation with curiosity, then we are students. The question is not, How do I make this unwanted situation go away? The question becomes, What is this situation asking me to learn?

Figure 8: Stuck practice, Eileen Fisher Learning Lab, New York, 2017.
Lynda Sing. Photo credit: Ricardo Dutra.

Stuck is not sustainable

One definition of something that is *sustainable* that appears in the Oxford English Dictionary is "a process or enterprise able to be maintained or continued while avoiding the long-term depletion of natural resources." Stuck causes a depletion of natural resources. Nature is never stuck but is always fluid and moving. Everything changes, gives birth, transforms, shifts, fades, dies. Fixation is unnatural. Unnatural is unsustainable.

Stuck knows what to do next

To learn from this practice, cultivate an attitude of not knowing what will happen. Our thinking brain does not know what the stuck shape wants to do. It does not know where the body wants to move or what shape will end the movement. But the physical body or the social body *does* know what to do. By making the stuck shape visible and taking the time to really feel that shape, we experience how and where the stuck shape wants to move. We listen to the body. We let go of knowing what we think we want. We let go of planning, fixing, manipulating. We don't think about it or try to figure it out. We don't *try* to do anything. Instead, we pay attention to what our body wants to do, and then just follow that. Here is an example of using the Stuck practice in a client context.

Figure 9: Stuck practice, Eileen Fisher Learning Lab, New York, 2017. Lynda Sing. Photo credit: Ricardo Dutra.

Application of Stuck to an Organizational Collaboration on Antitrafficking

by Manish Srivastava

Human trafficking is the "recruitment, transportation, harboring or receipt of persons, by means of coercion, abduction, deception or abuse of power or of vulnerability, for the purpose of exploitation." Encompassed within the International Labour Organization's (ILO) definition of forced labor, human trafficking is a backbone of the $150 million generated yearly in illegal profits from forced labor in the private economy. Almost two-thirds ($99 billion) of that sum in 2014 was generated from commercial sexual exploitation, in which the majority of the 4.5 million victims were women and children.[5]

Kamonohashi is a Japanese nongovernmental agency working across South Asia and India with a commitment to creating a world without human trafficking. In India, Kamonohashi works with Save the Children India (and other local partners) to create an effective antitrafficking ecosystem. Recognizing that they differed in how to approach this complex systemic challenge, the two organizations tried many ways to resolve conflicts and improve their collaboration, with mixed results. They wanted to experiment with a different methodology. In 2017, Kamonohashi invited me to help them build a strong collaboration between the partners and to co-create an ecosystem that supported the draft of an antitrafficking bill in India.

After some dialogue interviews, we gathered a team of stakeholders at different levels from both organizations for a three-day workshop using Social Presencing Theater. Among other practices, we used Stuck to make visible how each person felt in the current situation. Participants embodied their struggles and asked other participants to embody forces that were keeping them stuck (Sculpture 1). Their move to Sculpture 2 then generated insights about how they could extract themselves and move forward from their current conflicts.

We took photographs of their sculptures and reflected on the organizational patterns. We asked what common patterns were keeping them stuck in this partnership. A few insights stood out: "Everyone in the room has similar Stuck patterns." "We are pulled in different directions." "We are bumping our heads against something." "The way out of the Stuck is often by letting go and letting fall our stand, ideas, beliefs." The Stuck activity helped generate compassion and allowed them to see their individual roles in co-creating the stuck system.

Six months later, I followed up with the teams. A shift had occurred in their relationship. When I asked what had led to the shift, one of the participants recalled that during the Stuck activity, when she moved her foot from between the two conflicting forces, they found a way to stand together in one direction (in Sculpture 2). It was a powerful insight for her. She later tried it out in her work by stepping back and letting other partners find their relationship. It worked. They were now working together after five years of impasse.

The Stuck practice and 4-D Mapping (explained in chapter 4) helped them to see how their focus on anti-trafficking and justice had created an ecosystem that was ignoring what the victims needed even more. One of the leaders reflected, "We assumed that working for justice would bring dignity to the girl. This practice made us realize that perhaps we are going wrong here. She longs to be accepted back into her community and find her dignity there!" Integrating the girls back into their communities was an idea that had not been explored but now influences the work of the organizations.

As a facilitator, I was humbled by the power of this work. While our mind longs for conflict resolution, our bodies help us dissolve altogether. By seeing and sensing the suffering of the field together, the teams released their stuck energy and found a renewed commitment to working together.

Figure 10: Kamonohashi–STCI Partnership Workshop, Khandala, India, 2017.

Reflections on Stuck

The Sculpture 2 shape—the emerging future—was dormant in Sculpture 1. At the beginning, both teams fixated on the surface difficulties, stuck in patterns of habit and discord that kept them from their true purpose and blocked innovative and beneficial engagement. Their full potential was covered over by confusion and conflict. But in the very embodiment of their difficulties were the seeds of the change they wanted to make. Both teams began to see in their Stuck sculpture ways in which they could co-create better working relationships between the organizations and new perspectives on working with the women and girls they served. Their future was hidden in their Stuck sculptures.

Sculpture 2 is not a utopia. Sometimes there is a tendency to identify Sculpture 1 as the embodiment of an unpleasant state of mind and then to think of, and head toward, a more pleasant Sculpture 2. We limit the learning or healing potential of the practice if we set these parameters. Awareness of our shifting states of mind while engaging in embodiment practice is certainly informative and beneficial; yet there are drawbacks if we frame this practice as "stuck to unstuck." Doing so would miss the full potential of the practice. The value here is not whether the experience is pleasant or unpleasant. It is in what we can learn about the truthful next step.

The Stuck shape embodies a situation in which we find ourselves. It has forces that are pressing or pulling on it. We attend with great interest to the moments of movement from the Stuck shape. For instance, a few minutes ago I stopped writing, got up from my chair, and created a Stuck shape that embodied a current blockage in my writing process. I often do this—get up from my desk and do a short Stuck practice when I encounter a computer challenge or a barrage of emails. In this case I noticed that as I intensified my Stuck to make it more vivid, the feeling in my shoulders was not sustainable. The shoulders were the first part of my body to move. Shoulder movement allowed the arms and hands to move, the head and neck to shift attention. The front of my chest and heart area felt more protected; my gaze shifted from out to down. My knees bent, and my weight shifted more to one leg. As I rested in my Sculpture 2, the words that came out without thinking were "there is danger."

If I were using Stuck as a problem-solution method, I would probably say, "That's not a very cheerful outcome. The practice didn't work." Getting the desired outcome is very seductive. However, the point of the practice is to gain insight into possible next steps in a creative process. The insight for me from this Stuck and the words "there is danger" was about humility. Humility was a "message" from my Stuck. I do not know why this came to me, but I do know that some truth was uncovered that helps me move forward.

Over several months in 2018 I had the opportunity to do several Stucks with different groups around the same issue—a work pattern of mine that included too much travel. I felt stuck in this pattern and wanted to change it. After I created my Sculpture 1 shape, I asked two team members to pull strongly on my arms so that I felt off-center. Then I asked the third team member to sit next to me and hold down the foot that was serving as my home base. Although we do not share our individual stories or the names of any of the obstructing forces with others in the sculpture, I knew that the person holding down my foot embodied an intention to be at home and grounded in one place. In Sculpture 1, I could feel the strong pulling forces and the weak grounding force. Each time I set up this particular group Stuck with different groups, the same thing would happen. The person

Figure 11: Chalk drawings of Stuck. Credit: Agathe Peltereau-Villeneuve.

holding my foot would leave. She did not stay with me or apply more pressure to ensure that I had a reliable and strong home base. She would roll away or stand up and move to some other place in the sculpture. By Sculpture 2 she was nowhere near my foot. [See Fig. 11]

I had an agenda and a definite idea of a good outcome. I wanted the person holding my foot to remain steadfast in holding me close to home. I wanted insights about staying home. But that never happened. Instead I was invited into the truth of the journey from Sculpture 1 to 2. What was this shift from Sculpture 1 to 2 telling me? I could have made sense of this in different ways. The insight I took from it was that, for this period in my life, my colleagues, the social bodies that I worked with, were my home. I felt at home in the Sculpture 2 and at home with the teams I worked with. Shortly thereafter, when my colleague Julie Arts and I met for work in Shanghai, I actually said, "Seeing you feels like being home." My longing for a physical home lessened, and I began to feel more "at home" with colleagues, independent of place.

At the beginning of the Covid-19 pandemic, the Presencing Institute offered several online programs. In one of these sessions a woman in my small breakout group shared that something remarkable had happened in her Stuck. She said that the words that she spoke from her sculptures were insights that she did not know she had. She said these words had never crossed her mind but arose from the shape that her body made. She said that her words connected her with her own deeper understanding, which had been hidden.

It takes only a few minutes to create the body shape that we call Sculpture 1 and then to move with mindfulness from there into a second body shape, Sculpture 2. And yet when we place our attention on this activity, a knowing that had not previously surfaced in our conscious mind suddenly appears. We can do the practice individually, or we can build a group sculpture. In either case, words arise that are not planned or expected. They are what American poet Allen Ginsberg called "first thought, best thought."[6] He was referring to insights arising from the open space of the mind that can deepen self-knowledge, clarify a direction, or shift our perspective. These insights arise from our own body-mind integration, from the social field of our sculptures, and from the open space of the present moment. This quality of intelligence lives in us all and can be made accessible through this practice.

04

A LIVING SYSTEM SEES AND SENSES ITSELF: 4-D MAPPING

In 2010, before the first Presencing Global Forum in Cambridge, Massachusetts, Otto Scharmer proposed that we gather for two days with some colleagues from the dance world and the Presencing community. We were eager to include Jan Jacob Stam, Georg Senorer, and Maria Sturm, European senior practitioners of Organizational Constellations, a methodology for surfacing and healing deep historic patterns in individuals and organizations, developed from the work of German psychotherapist Bert Hellinger. We spent the time experimenting with a variety of movement improvisation forms and Constellations. This was during Occupy Wall Street in Boston—part of an international demonstration for social and economic justice and for democracy. Otto suggested that we make a map that embodied the voices of the global players that gave rise to the demonstration—forces that were the causes of inequality and that possessed the potential for change. He brought a chair to the center of the circle, stood up on it and said, "Banking." Jan Jacob stood next to him and said, "Multinationals." Beth Mount entered the space, sat off to the side, and said, "Mothers." Others entered adding roles, including education, religion, planet Earth, and change-makers. Georg entered last saying, "China."

Then we all began moving around. This lasted quite a long time—perhaps as long as twenty minutes. We eventually stopped and began talking about what had happened. That was the birth of 4-D Mapping. It was a blend of contemplative embodied presence practices, the Theory U process, Organizational Constellations, and a social change application. That night, Adam Yukelson and others stayed up making sets of name labels for the ten roles we had identified in the Occupy Wall Street mapping exercise. The following day, having done this only once, we invited the 250 participants to gather in groups of ten to engage in the practice. We called it 4-D Mapping—a process that would allow a larger system to see and sense itself.

Kurt Lewin, the founder of action research, is quoted as saying, "You cannot understand a system until you try to change it."[1] Otto follows up on that idea with two of his own reflections: "You cannot change a system unless you change consciousness," and "You cannot change consciousness unless the system can see and sense itself."[2] Lewin's statement reminds us of the futility of trying to change a system from the outside. The word system implies, for some of us, that it is outside of us—abstract and numbing. The health care system, the global financial system—each term suggests layer upon layer of structure, governance, power, values, decisions, culture, history. Racism, wealth inequality, and the destruction of natural resources are the result of systems' structures and beliefs.

How could we possibly see or sense the whole of it? Even within our own organizations it seems impossible to see the whole picture. It's much easier to imagine that others are causing the problem. "They" are the system, and we remain separate by holding on to our righteous indignation, cynicism, or apathy.

Peter Senge describes the essence of systems thinking: "People begin to consciously discover and account for how their own patterns of thought and interaction manifest on a large scale and create the very forces by which the organization then 'is doing it to me.' . . . A true systems philosophy closes the feedback loop between the human being, their experience of reality, and their sense of participation in that whole cycle of awareness and enactment."[3]

Social Presencing Theater invites us into the challenge of acknowledging that we are all co-creators of the systems in which we live. It invites us to stop looking at systems as "out there," as in "it is the system's fault," and to be humble enough to say that the system out there is living in me. I am part of the system. I contribute to the co-creation of it. I may have influence and be in a position of power, or I may not. However, in a systems approach we acknowledge that we all have influence. For example, as long as we buy food and eat, we cannot say that the food system is entirely "out there."

This approach to systems is the ground for 4-D Mapping, in which participants embody the stakeholders in a system to investigate how change happens, how social fields shift. Stakeholders in 4-D Mapping are individuals or groups of people who can effect change in the system, who are affected by changes in the system, or both. When we share a felt experience of the system, almost as though it were a living being, then we are in a position to recognize and support changes. We use our physical and spatial intelligence to inquire into forces and relationships in the system. The map makes visible both the structure and quality of feeling of the stuck system and also reveals the source of creativity and the potential for moving toward healthy and innovative possibilities.

As in the Stuck practice, 4-D Mapping investigates a short duration of time—from a starting sculpture to a second sculpture. 4-D stands for four dimensional, which in its simplest explanation means the experience of time. 2-D is a flat drawing; 3-D adds the depth dimension of space. 4-D indicates that a social field shift happens over time. Our interest is in the process by which social fields shift from ego orientation with the separate parts operating in their own bubble of reality, to ecosystem wholeness. We understand this more deeply by engaging in the journey from Sculpture 1 (current reality) to Sculpture 2 (the emerging future).

All of the elements in a 4-D Map are interconnected and dependent upon one another, even if this is not immediately apparent. The Iceberg Model helps us understand both the obvious and the less easily perceived layers of interdependence. It illustrates the relationship between symptoms on the surface and the web of deeper causes. Symptoms manifest as recognizable dysfunctions or stuck places in teams, organizations, and larger systems. Climate change, food insecurity, and wealth inequality are examples of global symptoms with multiple layers of causes and conditions. In the Iceberg Model, the symptoms above the waterline are the results of our collective actions. The underlying causes are less visible. The model helps us look below the surface of the water to understand that change needs to be activated on deeper levels in order to be sustainable and not simply a quick fix. 4-D Mapping is a process by which we can sense into and integrate these deeper ways of understanding.

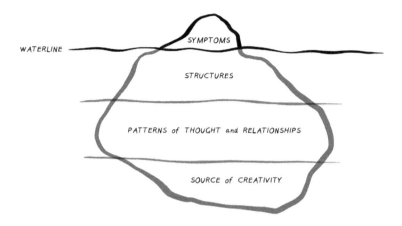

Figure 12: Iceberg Model. Drawing credit: Kelvy Bird.

Since 4-D Mapping is intended to investigate an existing societal or organizational situation, the process begins with a description of the symptoms of that situation. In 2020, a university student, Robin Duval, brought a case to a Social Presencing Theater workshop about the community of Govanhill, about fifteen minutes from the center of Glasgow, Scotland. In this historically working-class and migrant community, Robin told us, "New social enterprises are popping up on the high street, and new cycle paths into the city are being developed. There has been a community campaign to improve the quality of housing. Rent prices are increasing as more middle class young people move into the area attracted by lower rent prices and grassroots social events."[4] Robin was concerned about the relationship between those who had lived there for decades, primarily in government-subsidized housing administered by the local housing association, and the newcomers. The symptom: a lively revitalizing energy alongside increased housing insecurity for many who had lived their whole lives in the neighborhood.

Directly under the waterline lie structures. In an organizational Iceberg Model, all structures are not visible because of the complexities associated with governance, power, allocation of resources, regulations, and other factors. In 4-D Mapping, however, we use the model in a much more literal way. We refer to structures as the visible configuration of bodies in space—the physical body shape, placement, and activity of each person who chooses to embody an aspect of the system in the map. After Robin told the story, the workshop participants selected roles and arranged themselves to create a map that embodied the current situation in Govanhill. In their Sculpture 1, the roles were: Property Owner, Local Councillor, Church Community Worker, Zero-Waste Business Owner, Young Private Renter, Housing Association Worker, Elderly Man on pension who has lived in the area all his life, a Romani Girl with insecure housing, the Earth, and the highest aspiration, which Robin named Affordable Well-Being for All. Together they placed themselves in the space to create a social sculpture, a visible picture of the whole. Using the information in Robin's presentation, they built a structure that expressed the current situation.

The 4-D Map is a microcosm of the actual system as the participants experience it, not based solely on facts and figures. The visible structure is a physical embodiment of that system.

As the players embodying the Govanhill community slowly moved to their Sculpture 2, their journey was visible to themselves and to those of us who were witnesses. In their second sculpture, the Earth was close to the ground at the center of the sculpture. Extending in a line from the Earth were the Housing Association Worker, the Romani Girl, and the Elderly Man. They were close to the ground, either sitting or lying down, connected to one another. Standing at the end of the line near the Earth were Affordable Well-Being for All, the Local Councillor, and the Church Worker. To both those in the map and the witnesses, they looked like protector figures. Kneeling or bending forward, creating a triangle that was placed near the center of Sculpture 2 were the Young Private Renter, the Property Owner, and the Zero-Waste Business Owner.

We could clearly see the choices that were made—where people moved to, who was close to whom, who was in the center, who was on the periphery, who was low to the ground, and who was standing. These elements made up a moving physical sculpture that traveled from Sculpture 1 to Sculpture 2. At times during the shift from the first to second sculpture, the focus of several players narrowed, and they failed to see the whole structure. During these minutes, parts of the system remained unacknowledged, below the waterline (invisible). They were in a collective blind spot, even though they were in plain sight.

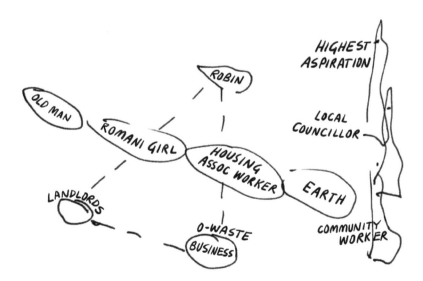

Figure 13: Sketch of Sculpture 2 from Robin's map. Drawing from Arawana's notebook.

The choices we make in a map (or in life, for that matter) are not solely based on what we see—the physical placement of people in space. Our choices are based on a feeling or sense about relationships. And this feeling or sense is influenced by paradigms of thinking. The Iceberg Model invites us to become aware of deeper, nonvisible levels that can both hinder healthy relationships and carry the potential for long-lasting positive change and profound innovation.

The quality of our relationships lies under structures. This intangible yet felt quality is inextricably linked to our thought patterns. Sometimes we hold mental models that limit a sense of connection and relationship.[5] Racism, for instance, is based on a mental model that fosters a disconnection from others who are different from us. Blaming others or being rigidly certain about how something should be, will diminish the quality of relationships. During our life we accumulate ideas, beliefs, and assumptions that shape how and what we notice and color how we regard ourselves and others. We express our ideas and feelings based on past experiences, often unconsciously, in the physical and spatial choices that we make.

In a 4-D Map the structures we create physically express thoughts, feelings, and how we relate to others. For example, in workshops at the 2014 Global Forum I saw several maps that included a role for immigrant women. In several maps, the participants who took this role placed themselves lying down in a curled position at the edge of the space. They sensed this role as excluded and without power. In another map a Latina took the role and placed herself standing, arms raised, in the middle of the space. Based on her experiences in her community, she chose to embody this role as fierce and central. In society these invisible qualities—thoughts and feelings—are enacted in decisions, policies, rules, buildings—in system structures.

And then, in turn, the structures influence how people think and feel.

There is no one way, no correct or incorrect way, of embodying a role. Each person has the agency to choose, based on their sense of the role. We choose shapes, spatial placement, and movement that express ideas, felt experience, and the relationships that role has with the others. As we move, we see clearly how our ideas and expectations influence how we feel and, in turn, the movement and spatial choices we make. Maps can reveal a painful sense of unintended disconnection. They illuminate choices made from unexamined interpretations and limiting assumptions. We appreciate everyone's choices. Maps are made for deep learning. We do not judge them as good or bad. We are not attached to outcomes. We use them to learn about the hidden aspects of the systems that we co-create. All maps hold some truth about a system, and all are regarded as expressing or showing movement forward toward deeper understanding and skillful action.

As players move from Sculpture 1 to Sculpture 2, the instructions are to let go of thoughts and opinions and simply to stay in the body and extend awareness to the whole, recognizing that the whole system is its own being. In the Govanhill community map we could sense the players tuning in to the quality of relationships. Positive regard grew as each player approached the others. The sense of the social field guided where they moved in the map. The process was subtle, but we could feel an increase in warmth and clarity as the movement progressed. The role-takers did not simply make conventional choices based on who they thought they should connect with or where they thought they should move. They made choices from an open-minded and open-hearted intention that clarified and deepened the quality of relationships in the social field as they journeyed from Sculpture 1 to Sculpture 2.

The 4-D Mapping process is a simplifying process that attends to an essential quality of how a system might move toward its aspirational self. The participants in Robin's map moved into their second sculpture based on a collective longing for clarity and a willingness to help Robin find a way forward for the community. By letting go of ideas and becoming aware of the whole, each found a place in relation to the others that expressed coherence and included all stakeholders.

The Iceberg Model holds an even deeper layer—the source of our collective creativity. Below the patterns of thought and relationships is a deeper source of humanness and innate creativity that is inherent in us all. Awareness, the open space of mind and heart, is the source of creativity. The practice invites us into this open space. We experience this system as a living, continually changing potential. When we experience the openness of possibility and a positive regard for every aspect of the system, then we have the courage to stay with the stuck patterns with loving attention and to allow them to transform into the compassionate systems that we know are possible.

This source of collective creativity is always present, often appearing where and when we least expect it. In the Govanhill map, several fresh insights arose from the group dialogue that followed the mapping process. Both the Elderly Man and the Romani Girl were close to the Earth, which gave Robin the idea that the park could play a vital role as a community gathering place. The triangle created by the young private renter, the zero-waste business, and the property owner opened a possibility that those three, who were in the position of being decision makers, might host inclusive community conversations on the topic of wellness for the whole community.

This map was the beginning of a process. Robin used 4-D Mapping to support research into how neighborhood renewal could increase social equality and also promote social change in the community. A second 4-D Mapping exercise on this same case at the Fire Starter Festival (run by Collective Leadership for Scotland in the Scottish government) uncovered the power dynamics between the property owner and the community.[6] This revelation gave rise to greater insights into the power of collective care as a basis for innovation.

> *The purpose is to transform collective interiors by first intentionally creating the "void" (blank sheet or empty stage to fill), and then "presencing" the new story or play that seeks to emerge, unconstrained by old habits and structural quagmires we've created. Not to focus on the result but put attention on the interior, the void that allows the full potential of any one of us or of any group to emerge. Physicalization of experience allows us to move from head to the truth of the body, our "holding space" for the sum of our senses and being. —Arawana's notebook entry from conversations with Otto Scharmer and others.*

The Three Divides

Every 4-D Map is an inquiry into a system within the larger global context. Although there are many people and organizations on the planet doing beneficial work, the magnitude of suffering on the planet is unfathomable. The challenges seem too great to overcome. There are many ways to try to make sense of the challenges we face as a global society. One approach that I have found helpful is what Otto calls the three divides—the ecological divide, the social divide, and the spiritual divide. We invite players to embody these three challenges in every 4-D Map.

The ecological divide expresses people's disconnection from the beauty, power, and wisdom of our natural environment. This lack of connection has desecrated the Earth, decreased our quality of life, and contributed to the loss of many precious species on our planet. Our collective consumption habits contribute to the degradation of our natural world and to the severe climate disruption that we experience today. So the Earth is a stakeholder in every map. The well-being of planet Earth is considered in every choice we make.

The social divide expresses the disconnection that we feel from one another in our global society. This inability to feel and care for others has produced massive social, racial, and economic inequality. The gap between those who have wealth and privilege and those who have neither is increasing.

Millions of people lack adequate food or clean water. Millions experience systemic oppression and violence. Those who do not have access to basic necessities, to education, and to opportunities are marginalized or excluded from the existing social systems. However, they are our sisters and brothers, stakeholders in the future, and they have a role in every map. Change comes from the margins of society—from youth like Swedish climate protection activist Greta Thunberg or Alicia Garza, Patrisse Cullors, and Opal Tometi, co-initiators of the Black Lives Matter movement. Our decisions must consider the well-being of those who have been excluded. I have heard that the Dalai Lama believes leaders must consider those on the planet who suffer the most in every decision that they make.

The spiritual divide expresses our disconnection from ourselves, from our spiritual wisdom and strength. When we lose the connection to our own basic goodness and to our highest aspirations and potential, we increase the number of people who suffer from depression, anxiety, burnout, despair, and suicide. The honesty in 4-D Mapping can reveal the shadow side and collective trauma of our systems and of ourselves. And yet each of us has an aspirational self, often unacknowledged, but present in every moment. Every map includes a role for our fullest potential and the highest aspiration of the system. Every 4-D Map includes the Earth, the Excluded, and our Highest Aspiration. We include them to feel the innate coherence in ourselves and the connectivity with other beings in our global family and with nature. Here is an example of how a colleague, Daniel Ludevig, used 4-D Mapping with a business client.

Application of 4-D Mapping
in a Banking Institution

by Daniel Ludevig

A critical European banking institution brought together its top leadership team of about thirty people to explore strategic options and its five-year plan. With the client open to doing a 4-D Mapping, I worked in advance of the workshop with a colleague, Hendrik Backerra, and the team's manager to identify the most relevant elements and stakeholders to include in the mapping. These included the internal roles: Leadership Team, Company Staff, and the various Committees within the organization. The list included external roles: Economic Markets, International Institutions, Internationally Minded People, People in Creditor Countries, and People in Borrower Countries. In addition, to embody the three divides, they chose the roles of Changing Environment (Earth), Immigrants (Excluded), and Stability and Success of the Euro (Aspirational Self).

As the mapping began, the participants sensed into the starting place and gesture for their chosen role (Sculpture 1). They then began their slow and tentative movements toward their second sculpture. Despite some initial skepticism, as they began to observe the movements around them a hush came over the group. Within seconds, it was as if all thirty people in the room became one body, noticing with both fear and recognition the dynamics that were playing out in front of them. After seven or eight minutes of movement, the participants arrived in their Sculpture 2 and began sharing their individual observations and experiences.

Those in the roles of the Leadership Team and the Company Staff were shocked at how inward their focus of attention had been throughout the mapping. The bank's Aspirational Self and Purpose, Stability and Success of the Euro, had felt entirely ignored. Adding to that, Immigrants and People in Borrower Countries had found themselves on the very edge of the room in which the map was unfolding. They were entirely out of sight of the key players who were huddled together in the center of the room moving around one another in circles for the majority of the journey from Sculpture 1 to 2.

After the mapping we engaged the group in a rich debrief around their observations, reflections, and interpretations of what had taken place. While many expressed sadness at the reality they had just experienced, there was also a new openness to recognizing their attention gaps. One participant mentioned that it reconnected him with the reason he had joined the bank in the first place. Another stated that she was shocked to see how accurately the mapping shed light on the dynamics and habits present in her system of work. The insights on strategic possibilities obtained from the visual and embodied dimension of these sculptures were so meaningful to the leadership team that they decided to use photos of Sculptures 1 and 2 to support their presentation of strategic options to the rest of the company. I have no doubt that the experience of the 4-D Mapping acted as a cornerstone for their development of a stronger foundation together, and consequently, a more fully lived purpose.

Practice and Reflection Instructions

Sit on chairs in a large circle. The facilitator will have prepared in advance the name of each stakeholder role (this process is not described here), with each name written on a card.[7] The facilitator calls the name of the first role. If you feel some resonance with that role, stand, walk into the circle, receive the card, clip it to your shirt, and choose where to place yourself in the space—for instance, in the center or at the periphery. Create a body shape that communicates your sense of the role. Choose a level: standing, sitting, or lying down. Choose which direction to face, knowing what is in your line of sight. Once in your shape and in your place, let one sentence come to mind that expresses your experience, and say that. A scribe records the sentence.

The facilitator calls the second role. If you feel resonance with the role, enter the circle, find your shape and place, and speak your sentence. This continues until all the stakeholder roles have entered the map and spoken. In this way you create a Sculpture 1 that embodies the current reality of that system.

Then collectively go through a condensed U process, as was described in the Stuck practice. The instruction is always the same: stay in the body, be aware of the whole, pay attention to the social field. Let go of thinking. Let go of planning. Let go of any expectation or idea about the outcome. Move for a few minutes, allowing the movements to arise from an embodied presence, awareness of the whole space, and a sense of the social field. Then pause in a second shape—Sculpture 2. From there, one by one, say the name of your role and one sentence that embodies your Sculpture 2 shape or your journey from Sculpture 1 to 2.

Both the players and the citizens reflect on the process—first on the particular moments in the map, using "I saw," "I felt," "I did," and then in generative conversation. Generative conversations are spacious, allowing insights, innovation, and shared inspiration to arise.[8]

A series of questions can guide the dialogue process:

What touched you?

Where did the movement begin?

What did you see or experience that confirmed what you already believed to be true?

What surprised you?

What did you see or experience that was disconfirming?

How are Sculptures 1 and 2 different?

Where did you notice a shift in the social field?

Where do you see seeds of possibility and possible prototype opportunities?

If a client has requested the map, then the facilitator invites their reflections on what they learned and how this might inform them going forward. Conclude with a closing ritual for stepping out of the map.

Figure 14: 4-D Mapping done by advanced training practitioners, New York, 2017. Photo credit: Ricardo Dutra.

4-D Mapping heightens observation skills. Participants notice spatial arrangements and patterns—circles, overcrowded places, and level changes. They notice lines of energy and connection. Were some roles ignored? Was there any inversion of power? Did those in the center remain in the center and those on the margins remain on the margins? Did anyone lying or sitting on the floor move to standing? Did anyone who stood alone move to join others, or vice versa? The mapping process develops literacy in embodied language that supports our noticing the connections between the roles in the map.

All living beings and the natural world itself are intimately connected. We have an inner knowing that what happens in one part of our living system affects us all. And yet we do not always experience this connection or live from this knowing. It is easy to forget and to live as though our actions are independent from those of others. Separating from this fundamental truth of interconnection produces suffering. In 4-D Mapping we directly experience the interdependency of all the stakeholders in the system.

However, this interdependency does not preclude our own sense of agency. The key is awareness and care for the whole. In 4-D Mapping we do not interfere with other people's choices. After introducing the roles, the facilitator doesn't intervene in the process. The facilitator never interrupts a mapping process to comment on or direct any action. The transition from Sculpture 1 to Sculpture 2 is an unbroken ceremony with its own form and integrity. Those witnessing do not get up from their chairs and join the players. Participants cannot manipulate the bodies of others. For instance, they cannot lift a person from sitting to standing, or put their hands on another's shoulders to point that person to another place. They cannot direct two people to join hands. Each person moves freely, allowing the social field to find its own movement.

We shift from depending on our conceptual and intellectual learning and interpretation to the knowing that is in the body and in the space. We let go of thinking that we know what should happen or what we want to happen. By trusting in the body-knowing and in the intelligence that lives in the space, we begin to experience this collective sculpture as a being, as its own entity, not simply as a collection of individuals. It is its own being that seems to have its own life, its own pattern and rhythm, if we just stop trying to control it. We can relax a little and let this being express its own sorrow, sanity, and beauty.

We can sense a longing to connect with the basic health and wholeness already present in our experience as we move from Sculpture 1 to Sculpture 2. Underlying every Sculpture 1 that models the current state of each system is basic goodness and the potential to sense and connect with it. When we let go of conventional, reactive responses to conflict, confusion, or unhealthy power dynamics, we sense sanity under the surface. Under all that appears, is there a source of well-being?

Application of 4-D Mapping
to Systems Transformation in Cambodia:
Youth-Led Collaborative Venture Lab

by Manish Srivastava

In 2018, the Presencing Institute worked with the Development Coordination Office within the Office of the UN Secretary General to pilot the SDG Leadership Lab in Cambodia. In 2016, the United Nations members adopted the seventeen Sustainable Development Goals (SDGs) to achieve a better world for people and the planet by 2030. A key element of the Cambodia process was the Youth-Led Collaborative Venture Lab, which brought together leaders from UN agencies and from government, business, and civil society, along with Cambodian youth representatives, to generate a cross-sectoral partnership road map for addressing the challenges faced by youth in Cambodia. As facilitators, our role was twofold: to help this diverse group of leaders see and sense the systemic challenges together, and to support their development of partnerships and projects.

A few weeks before the lab, we formed a design team of young leaders within UN Cambodia. The team interviewed all youth stakeholders and invitees and summarized their reflections into one question: What would empower youth to learn, earn, and contribute to sustainable development in Cambodia?

We then asked them to identify ten roles of stakeholders who mattered most for transforming the ecosystem supporting youth in Cambodia. We guided them to keep the three divides (ecological, societal, and spiritual) in mind while selecting roles. While facilitating the 4-D Mapping, I was a bit skeptical that such a diverse group would engage effectively with an embodiment-based creative process. To my surprise, Social Presencing Theater provided them a method to make visible their collectively felt reality beyond the limitations of sectoral, generational, and gender divides.

As we mapped the current reality in Sculpture 1, the systemic divides became visible and evident to all. Everyone in the room was quiet and fully tuned in.

As we moved from Sculpture 1 to Sculpture 2, clusters emerged among the roles, crystallizing the potential places where collaborations could be fostered to transform the ecosystem.

Figure 15: 4-D Mapping at the Youth-Led Collaborative Venture Lab, a multi-stakeholder co-creation process organized by UN Cambodia.

After initial reflection, we asked participants to identify places in the map that had the most potential to shift the ecosystem. They identified six such venture areas. We then formed six cross-sectoral teams to develop change prototypes based on the insights generated from the map. Over the next twelve months the teams experimented with the prototypes and shared their learning with each other.

Here is one example of an outcome from their 4-D Mapping. Participants noted that when Social Enterprises and Business came together in the map, their attention shifted to the Youth. An insight arose in the group that those two groups could work together toward inclusive development. A prototype idea was born to create an SDG Business Award for local businesses that partnered with youth representatives.

Participants said that 4-D Mapping helped them to see and sense the whole system together and to create collaborations on what mattered most. It also transformed the intergenerational dynamics between youth leaders and institutions. Fabienne Moosmann, UNFPA youth coordinator in Cambodia, shared this observation at the end of workshop: "I'm not sure what the future holds, but after this week, I know young people in Cambodia will have a say and they will have the space to lead."

I am grateful to UN leaders, including Pauline Tamesis, Ifoda Abdurazakova, and the United Nations Country Team (UNCT), as well as to the Presencing Institute facilitation team, including Becky Buell, Katie Stubley, and John Stubley, for co-creating this experience.

Maps help us sense more deeply into a system, and they reveal seeds of the future—potential prototypes. In Daniel's description of the bank's 4-D Mapping experience, deep sensing into the organization's collective patterns was an essential outcome of the map. Manish's maps in the antitrafficking and Cambodian youth practices emphasized leverage points for action. In all three cases connections and patterns appeared that the participants were able to use to create prototypes. Seeds of the future are embedded in every map. They can be picked up, planted, and exposed to sunlight energy and nurturing moisture. The practice invites us to deepen our experience of the present moment, access the future that wants to unfold, contemplate our own role, and then act. We can invite two people who stood next to one another in the map to a meeting. We can email or call someone, learn about something, create a model. We act without hesitation.

Brokenheartedness

Losing a sense of connection to our creative selves and to others creates suffering. We all experience large and small suffering daily. Our inability to control the ups and downs of life can cause anxiety. Many of us who call ourselves change-makers are often not comfortable with change. I want things to work out. I hope pleasant experiences will remain and fear they will not. I want good results in my 4-D Mapping and in life. 4-D Mapping is a good opportunity to practice equanimity in the midst of ever-changing and uncontrollable circumstances.

Confusion and a longing to connect lived in the three stories presented in this chapter. The actual mapping was only half of the process. The other half was reflecting and engaging in open conversation about the experience. The conversation generated shared meaning, insights, and possible steps forward. Sometimes, as in Daniel's case description of the bank's experience, Sculpture 2 produces a more painful outcome than the participants expected.

I need to say something about this, since I sometimes hear people say, "Our map didn't work. We did not get a good result." Sometimes the journey from Sculpture 1 to Sculpture 2 reveals deeper layers of disconnection than were evident at first. People sometimes make choices that they think will lead to more harmony or more coherence, and the effect of their choices is the opposite of the intention. As we saw with the bank, some stakeholders can be ignored, excluded, or controlled by others. We sense in the map what we experience in our organization or in society.

Still, there is value in the Sculpture 2 maps that don't, on the surface, seem to produce a good outcome. The map is not a crystal ball. It is not a solution to a problem. It creates an opportunity for reflection and learning. Sensing more deeply into a system can, and frequently does, reveal hidden patterns of thought and relationships that are more conflicted than what appeared on the surface. In a mapping done several years ago in the US for a national youth leadership development organization, the role of a Black youth became more and more isolated during the movement from the first sculpture to the second. Those of us sitting in the circle, witnessing and holding the space, watched painfully as the choices made by well-meaning players collectively created a pattern of exclusion for the young person.

We see in this practice how difficult it is to let go of our projections and conventional beliefs. We see our collective blind spots. We see this in maps of business organizations, school systems, nongovernmental organizations, and in the heartbreaking situation of refugees and migrants. In all maps, patterns of habitual absencing appear, as well as moments of wakeful presencing. We have become aware of how frequently we see the same patterns of not noticing, of unhealthy power dynamics, and of conventional reactiveness, no matter what system we are mapping. From deeply engaging in one system, we gain insights into other systems and the larger web of interconnection in which we live.

The longing for a good society and the sense of basic goodness embedded in the system accompanies—lives side by side with—the anguish we feel about the cruelty, stupidity, and greed that cause untold suffering. Individual and collective suffering and trauma have always existed. Tragedy has always been part of the human condition. Today, however, we see the social sculptures of injustice and abuse daily and cannot avoid brokenheartedness.

Sadness is a strong motivating force for change. In almost every 4-D Mapping that I have experienced, poignancy or sadness appears. We experience the frustration in the system as deep sadness. It is heartbreaking to be human. We have so much longing for a good world for our children and their children, on into the future. And yet we see that each of us plays a role in keeping the system stuck, in co-creating results that none of us wants. We see how we produce suffering for ourselves and for others. In the 4-D Mapping, we feel that tenderhearted sadness. In the example above where we experienced the marginalization of the Black youth in the mapping exercise, the reflective conversation following the mapping process was extremely painful. Why did this happen? Why did we make choices that created violence in the young person and confusion for us all? Some members of the group wanted to do another map. They wanted another outcome. We all sat in silence. Then a man in the group spoke. He said that the outcome was collective grief and that staying with and going more deeply into that feeling was in itself the outcome that they needed.

When we can collectively stay with a feeling of deep sadness, it has power as a motivating force for change. The key here is to stay with the feeling without trying to push it away, rationalize it, pathologize it, or judge it. In my own tradition of Shambhala, sadness is a code word for compassion. Compassion can sometimes have a high-falutin', better-than-others implication. But sadness is down-to-earth, tenderizing, and powerfully human. It can get us moving out of our comfort zone, out of our privilege, out of self-protection, into the completely messy business of actually helping our world.

05

CULTIVATING AN EMBODIED PRESENCE: THE 20-MINUTE DANCE

Recently I met a woman who said, "I work as a hospital administrator, and I usually live in my head. In u.lab I discovered that people applying Theory U in organizations are actually bringing in this body stuff. I cannot imagine using my body. Where would a person like me start?"

The starting point is easy. Always start with yourself—noticing and cultivating your own embodied presence. Embodied presence enables us to simply be. Simply being is an unconditional sense of all rightness for no reason—not because of credentials, not because of circumstances, but just because we are humans standing on this good Earth beneath the sky, this is enough. This experience is basically good. We are simply being.

The journey begins by connecting to the Earth beneath us. Feeling connected to the ground supports being present. Feeling grounded, not floating around in the thought world, is a foundation for cultivating the experience of simply being. Being present in this moment of life, sitting in a chair, is enough. It is enough to feel our human-beingness. A sense of being supports an experience of well-being. When our attention rests in the body, we can begin to settle down. The feeling can be pleasurable or painful. We do not need to label our experience as good or bad. It simply is. We know that this is our genuine experience, and we can settle into that without judgment, with appreciation and curiosity. A grounded person is trustworthy and available. Others feel that.

When you walk down the hall, do you feel grounded? Do you feel your body walking, or are you lost in thought? Are you simply pushing your body ahead to your destination, thinking about something that happened yesterday? Do you feel your feet contacting the floor? You might wonder why these questions are important. You might think that the whole point of walking is to get somewhere. Why attend to each footstep when you could be thinking about important things? This work of embodied presence will put a speed bump into rushing toward a specific destination. It values the moment-to-moment sensory experience, which will require some slowing down. What is the experience of this moment of walking?

> Walk at an ordinary pace, but feel each foot as it touches the floor, and feel the rest of your body connect to the earth. There is no need to walk very slowly. You don't want to call attention to your action if others are around.

> Likewise, notice yourself sitting when you are in front of the computer, with others, or eating lunch. Just notice that you are sitting down on a spot on the planet. There is no need to perch. You can relax, let go of any thoughts, and let your weight sink down into the chair.

In embodiment practice, we bring our attention to the sensations of the body—the shape of the body sitting in the chair, the sense of the body's weight. We might notice that the body is breathing and that it feels a certain way. If we were sitting in another chair, in another posture, in another place in the room, it would feel different. We draw our mind away from the constant habit of fixating on thoughts. We let it rest on the feeling of the body—in this case, sitting in a chair. The mind rests in the body; the body rests in a chair on the big Earth body. This connection between our body and the Earth body is important to our general sense of being. Just for a moment, we can let go of our agenda and simply be.

The 20-Minute Dance invites us into a world of body awareness and embodied presence. It is a user-friendly beckoning: attend to the body; feel the natural harmony between the body and the mind. There are no new movements to learn or remember, and there is no way to improve or fail. We use mindfulness, the mind's ability to pay attention, as a method for experiencing the synchronization between the body and mind. We call this body-mind coherence "embodied presence." It is living fully in the body that we have and appreciating ourselves just as we are. It is noticing that the body and mind (our attention) are naturally synchronized.

Sometimes we notice that our body and mind behave like an estranged couple living in the same house but only talking to each other when necessary. In fact, the mind can be quite aggressive toward the body and make severe demands on it. We are frustrated and angry when it breaks down, gets sick, doesn't work, fails to meet our expectations. The body becomes an "it" with which we are either pleased or displeased. Or sometimes we just forget the body. We are so much in our heads, attached to our thoughts, that we do not taste our food or "feel" our family members. Sometimes people tell me that they don't feel their body. This is probably a bit of an exaggeration, but we know what they mean. With the demands of daily life, many of us need a designated time each day to simply come into the body in an easy and natural way—to let our body and mind remember their innate integration. We let ourselves simply be.

Start on the ground

One of the simplest and quickest ways to feel grounded is to lie down on the ground. Most of us are indoors when we practice the 20-Minute Dance, but we can still feel the solidity and depth of our Earth. (Lying down on the ground outside would be even better.) In chapter one, I referred to three bodies: the individual body, the Earth body, and the social body. The 20-Minute Dance connects our individual body with the Earth body. Lying down allows much of our body surface to contact the floor. Lying there we feel our place in the room, our place on the planet. Every being—persons and other beings—has a spot on the planet right now. We can experience our spot, our place on the Earth. We can feel settled there. We feel our Mother Earth body holding us close. She holds on to us so that we don't float off into space. She is a completely trustworthy support. We can feel nourished by her resources and wealth. Water, oil, gold, silver, jewels, the roots of plants and trees, the ashes of our dead—all are on our Earth. We can feel the truth—that we are part of this Earth and that we belong. We can rest in that feeling.

Shift attention from thinking to feeling

The 20-Minute Dance invites us to shift our attention away from thinking to feeling, away from what we are thinking about to specifically what we are feeling in the body. The language of the body is feeling or sensation, and this practice is an invitation to listen to the body's voice. The word *feeling* doesn't refer to emotion, as in feeling

Practice and Reflection Instructions

Begin the 20-Minute Dance by lying down on the floor. Let go of thoughts and shift your attention from thinking to feeling the body. Attending to the feeling of the body, alternate between moving and stillness. Attend to the feeling in a part of the body where there is sensation, or to an overall sense of the whole body. Follow what the body wants to do. When thoughts arise, let them go and return your attention to the feeling of the body in this moment.

During the twenty-minute practice time, gradually move from lying down to sitting up, then rise to standing, and then move about in the room. End the practice by resting in a final standing shape. Take a few minutes to reflect on your experience or write in a journal. Simply recollect what you did and how that felt.

angry. We simply notice how the body feels, the physical sensations—either in a part of the body or with a sense of the whole body. This could be colored by an emotion; but we do not focus on that.

In order to attend with care to the body, we invite some quietness of mind. We let go of thoughts. Thinking, whether it is about the body or about something else, is not the same as experiencing or feeling the body. In fact, constant thinking is what keeps us separated from the feeling of the body. So, in this practice we lighten up on our thinking and establish a habit of staying in the body, developing loyalty to the body.

Sensing, opening our sense perceptions, is one of the primary capacities we use to engage in a U process of change. We attend to the feeling of the body to build capacity for sensing, for deepening the body-knowing capacity that we need to establish healthy relationships with ourselves, with others, and with the natural world around us. Neither embodiment nor embodied presence was likely to have been in our school curriculum, and today many of us need support in bringing this body intelligence into our everyday experience. We cannot relate fully with the complexity of our lives today by thinking more, thinking faster, or being more brainy. We cannot understand the challenges we are facing by only looking at facts. We also need to tap into this underutilized resource called the sensing body.

Value doing nothing

We spend half of our practice time in *non*doing, resting in body shapes. The body is waiting, listening, hanging out. We rest in the space of still-body. Then still-body gives birth to a movement. It will, after a time, feel inclined to move. We are curious about what the body wants to do next. If we give our planning, manipulating, ambitious, improvement-oriented mind a rest, we can let the body simply do what it wants. We are interested in knowing what it wants to do when we stop controlling it. The 20-Minute Dance is a restorative-justice opportunity. We invite the voice of the controlling mind to step back in order to let the voice of the sensing body step forward. Sometimes the body yells at us through painful sensations or extreme tension or dis-ease. But often the body's voice has been silenced, and here we invite the quiet, subtle voice of the body to be heard. We do what the body wants to do, not what our thinking mind wants to do. Just for twenty minutes we can relax our mind in order to listen to the body.

Apply mindfulness

The 20-Minute Dance trains the mind to attend to the feeling of the body using mindfulness. The practice of mindfulness engages an object—a place to rest our attention. For instance, we can walk mindfully or eat mindfully, which means we attend to what we are doing without becoming distracted by thoughts or by our cell phone. In the 20-Minute Dance, we rest our attention on the body in order to remember that we have a body, and that, in fact, we live there. In Tibetan the word *mindfulness (trenpa)* translates as "to remember, to recollect." But it does not refer to remembering something in the past. When we are mindful, we remember the present moment and its complete fullness. Our body and mind are an amazing system, innately synchronized, but we forget this. We are often so caught in memories of the past or imaginings of the future that we forget to experience the present moments of our life. Mindfulness practice invites us to remember.

Mindfulness works like this: We place our attention on the experience of our body. This could be a sensation in some part of the body—the shoulder, for instance. Or we could have a sense of our whole body, how our whole system hangs together. We are not focusing or concentrating. We lightly place our attention and let it rest there. Then a thought arises. It could be a thought about anything: "This reminds me I should go back to yoga class," or "I wish I could get this neck pain to go away." Our natural, innate, everyday awareness notices that these are thoughts. Awareness itself does not have an opinion or judgment about what we are thinking. It just notices. And it knows that thinking about something is not the same as feeling the body. The noticing reminds us to let thoughts go and to re-place our attention on the body. It is a gentle process of softening around a habit of continuous thinking. We repeat this process in an easygoing way as we practice moving and being still. Our practice is to rest our attention in our body, drift into thought, notice that we are thinking, gently place our attention on the body again, and let it rest there. Again and again.

We are not using mindfulness to correct, fix, or improve anything. We begin with the premise that our body-mind system is good just as it is. Shunryu Suzuki Rōshi, author of *Zen Mind, Beginner's Mind*, told his students, "Each of you is perfect the way you are ...and you can use a little improvement."[1] By appreciating ourselves just as we are, we develop an attitude of nonaggression toward our bodies and ourselves. We are at ease with ourselves. By simply becoming more and more familiar with our own body-mind and the subtle shifts that we experience moment by moment, change happens organically. "Improvement" is a natural process, not manipulated or forced. We naturally begin to prefer embodying the moments of our life. We are not trying to change. As we attend to our moment-by-moment experience, change unfolds naturally.

Attending to the details of our unfolding experience keeps us real, keeps us from conceptualizing our experience. It keeps us from constructing notions about our experience—interpretations based on the past. Attending, with directness and simplicity, to the details of our experience enables us to celebrate the beauty of each moment of our life.

Drop agendas and appreciate everything

Peter Senge talks about the importance of sometimes having agenda-less meetings—meetings that just meander where they want to go. The 20-Minute Dance is a lightly structured meandering in which we are not trying to accomplish anything. Not trying to improve ourselves or fix anything, we cultivate a friendly interest in how the body feels and what it wants to do next. There is no goal, nothing to accomplish. It's such a relief to give up trying to control or manipulate our experience, to not judge whether the experience is good or bad, whether it is right or wrong. We are simply being with the body and appreciating everything.

After doing my 20-Minute Dance today, I wrote in my journal: Before I could walk and run, I learned how to stand. Before I could stand, I learned how to sit. Before I could sit up, I was close to the ground as a crawler and creeper. After I entered the world, I lay on my back in a crib only able to move my limbs in the air. I wonder if I will leave the world in the reverse order. Already, I can barely run. One day I will discover I can no longer walk, then no longer stand.

The body is the reminder of change—of continual change and impermanence. The mind may gain insight, wisdom, and compassion over a lifetime, but the body ages, weakens, and reminds us of our own short time on this Earth. The 20-Minute Dance brings me into the ephemeral nature of body and life. The practice reminds me to appreciate this body just as it is.

Delight in not knowing what comes next

The ground of creativity is not knowing what comes next and delighting in that. The true move arises from this open space. The 20-Minute Dance is a practice in not knowing what comes next. We suspend the habit of manipulating, planning, figuring it out, doing what we should do, and so on. We are completely interested in attending to the present moment and what might happen next. We can relax and just let the body do whatever it wants within the minimal parameters of moving and stillness, from the ground to standing. We relax into "nothing much is happening." This nothingness provides a space for developing a sense of an emerging future. Not knowing is the space for innovation. It is the space from which surprises can arise. The late Michael Blumenstein, a colleague and practitioner of Organizational Constellations, once said, "In my everyday life, my movement is like driving down a highway, but in the 20-Minute Dance, I go off the highway on to the unfamiliar, small side roads and continuously discover new things about my body and about myself."

Remember your back

When we near the end of our twenty-minute practice time, we stand. It is good to feel the back of the body. When I work with groups, I sound a little like a broken record about this—remember your back. I first learned this as a dancer. Feeling the back of the body changed my posture, but more important, it opened my sense of spatial awareness. Back awareness gives the body a full 360-degree presence and supports awareness of our whole spatial context. If we lose touch with our back we over-focus on the front of the body and whatever is in front of us—what we can see with our eyes. This makes sense, of course. We face front, literally. Our face and sense organs face front. Our arms reach more easily to the front than to the back. We walk forward. All this contributes to a sense of the body as a *bas relief*—a sculpture that has only a front with a flat background. However, the body is not only a front. I have found that remembering my back brings me in touch with the strength of the back body, allowing the front to feel more open. And the sense of 360-degree embodiment brings an awareness of the space around me, the sides and the back.

Of course, we do need to attend to the people and things we see in front of us; however, this back aware-ness keeps us sensitive to the environment and atmo-sphere of our present moment. We have a sense of what or who is beside us, accompanying us, maybe going in the same direction that we are. Without actually seeing with our eyes what or who is behind us, we can sense the space behind. In my own case, I vividly feel support, both from my own spine and from the presence of all those who are backing me up, or who "have my back." I can imagine pro-tectors—my ancestors, teachers, and all the brave women and men in the past whose lives were devoted to creating a good world. They are always at our backs—always saying "Never give up" and cheering us on. I can imagine that they are standing behind us all.

When we are only aware of our front, we might lean forward, as though we are pitched forward. When we look at sculptures and paintings of leaders, such as Egyptian pharaohs, Chinese empresses, or Ooni rulers, we see that they are not leaning forward, trying to connect. Their dignity is expressed in the presence of the backs of their bodies and heads. We experience their strength. When we see images of the Buddha, he is not perched at the edge of his lotus seat. He sits upright, balanced in the middle. We can clearly sense the gentle strength and panoramic awareness in the image. Human dignity is expressed by a presence of the back. Once, a long time ago, a teacher said to me, "Your spine is where you live. Stay home." Remembering this allows me to simply be.

Supporting Awareness-Based
Change Work

*The success of an intervention depends
on the interior condition of the intervenor.*

—Bill O'Brien, former CEO of Hanover Insurance

*Anybody can play. The note is only 20 percent.
The attitude of [the one] who plays it is 80 percent.*

—Miles Davis, American jazz trumpeter and composer

The complexity of the challenges we face as a society requires a new level of personal and collective awareness. Becoming aware is the key, and therefore we engage in practices that cultivate our "interior condition"—mind, heart, and will. The global Covid-19 pandemic forced us to become vividly aware of our connections to one another—the shared uncertainty, grief, and concern for others. In the United States the pandemic, political chaos, and social unrest made it impossible for us to forget our country's inequality and racial injustice. The moment we saw in the media the social sculpture of George Floyd being murdered by law enforcement officers, our collective consciousness shifted. We could not turn away or pretend that it hadn't happened. What many of us knew but remained distant from became a vividly felt embodied awareness. This collective awareness is the basis for the understanding and courage that is required to make the needed change.

In awareness-based social change efforts, we emphasize the interior condition of those who are trying to bring about change, those who are using the methods and tools. In order to use the tools effectively, we need our full genuine presence. When we are aware of our full body-mind system, we can sense into our context with more precision and intervene more skillfully. Our perceptions are clear. There is inner coherence between our mind, our body, and our environment or context. We engage with genuineness. Genuineness is one of our greatest assets.

We experience in the 20-Minute Dance how shifting our attention to the feeling of the body pulls us out of the world of thinking, landing us in the present moment, in our own genuineness. The practice creates a longing to feel our feet on the ground and to get in touch with this underutilized resource—the body's intelligence. What we experience in our practice influences our everyday life. When we notice that we are caught in judgment or opinion, we gently bring our attention to the body. Returning to and listening to the body becomes a natural and integrated part of our everyday life. We ask, what does the body have to say about this? Our work demands that we bring our full presence and attention, including our body-knowing, to our experience. We need our full humanness.

Those of us who work with groups often start meetings with a "check-in." Each person shares something about how they are that day. When I worked in the theater, we began every rehearsal or performance with a warm-up. We checked in with ourselves: What kind of body is showing up today? How is my mind? How is my voice? And then we engaged in practices that tuned and toned our instrument. We engaged in the ritual of preparing body, speech, and mind so we could extend our best attention to the others in the ensemble and to the audience. I often wonder why in theater, which many would say is not real life, we put so much care into preparing to work, when in real life we often begin our workday without this preparation.

There are many wonderful embodiment practices available. Martial arts practitioners such as Richard

Strozzi-Heckler and Wendy Palmer bring aikido into the field of leadership. Thousands have shared practices online at the Embodiment Conference, and many people integrate both traditional and newly created methods into personal and social change efforts. We aspire to contribute to this stream of activity with Social Presencing Theater. Over the years I have had the privilege of studying body practices with remarkable teachers—yoga at Integral Yoga Institute, tai chi chuan with T. T. Liang, and qigong with Eva Wong. These practices have informed my life. But over the past four decades I have practiced the 20-Minute Dance most consistently. I cannot remember where it came from—maybe from the time that I worked with Jamie Cunningham in New York. The 20-Minute Dance has become my check-in around health, presence, and creativity.

Health

The 20-Minute Dance invites me to tune in to the body in a simple, nonjudgmental way to support my health—both physical and emotional. I can get so caught up in the demands of work and life that I do not realize I am coming down with a cold. I can keep at bay the fact that I need sleep, am overeating, or am dehydrated. I can ignore a stiff neck for months. I and many of us need designated time to actually feel how we feel—both in our bodies and in our minds. I have done 20-Minute Dances in which I begin to cry as soon as I lie down. I don't even realize that I am holding sadness in the body, but tears come and that sadness naturally integrates into my being and hydrates my heart-mind.

Many people have shared with me how the simple daily practice of the 20-Minute Dance has profoundly contributed to their sense of well-being, even their sanity. For most people, the practice is pleasurable. In spite of the discomfort that many of us live with from stress, injuries, or aging, it actually feels good to lie down on the floor and let the body do whatever it wants with no agenda, no goal, no right or wrong. It feels good and honest to simply appreciate the body that we have, even with its aches and pains. It feels good to give the body our attention, to listen to it, to feel that we are coming home. We live in the body; it is our home. It is good to come home every once in a while.

Over the years I have met people for whom establishing a friendly relationship with their body was difficult. It is well known that dancers and athletes often push their bodies in ways that are detrimental to their well-being. For others, through childhood or collective trauma, health issues, social image, or for other reasons, the body can become a foreigner, even an enemy, and it may take some time to make friends with it. Being with the body can be an unpleasant or frightening experience for some of us. There are many resources on somatic healing of individual and collective trauma, among them the work of Bessel van der Kolk, Peter A. Levine, and Resmaa Menakem.[2] We can learn to work with painful feelings around racism, gender identity, and conflict as we journey toward understanding and integration. Some of us need additional help to establish trust in our bodies.

The 20-Minute Dance offers the time, the space, and the possibility of settling into a nonaggressive and friendly relationship with the body. We benefit from letting go of the judgments, criticisms, dislikes, and disappointments related to our bodies. When we do the practice regularly we become gentler and kinder to our bodies. We go about life with basic coherence between our body and mind. We appreciate our own genuineness, which brings a deep sense of being and well-being.

I have done thousands of 20-Minute Dances over these past forty-plus years and have witnessed thousands of people practicing, and I have never seen or heard anyone use that twenty minutes to become more uptight, more distressed, or more dis-eased. People move toward what is a little more easeful, a little more open, and personally more coherent. Given some time and little structure, people go toward health and the natural synchronization of body and mind. We could hypothesize that since the body-mind system naturally wants to move toward health and integration, maybe this is true of social systems as well. Maybe the innermost longing of families, teams, organizations, and communities is to move toward a sense of wholeness and health. If so, what are the conditions that would enable this movement to happen?

Presence

We can see and feel when the people we are speaking with are grounded in their bodies. We can feel whether they are connected to the Earth and present to their own feelings. And we can tell when we are around "talking heads" who are disconnected from body, from "earthiness," from the deeper sense of knowing. We can feel that hollowness in ourselves and in others. Settling into the body brings a natural sense of simplicity and clarity. We can be more in touch while sitting in meetings, standing in front of clients, walking to our car. We begin to notice more, appreciate the changing colors of the leaves or the emotional resonance behind a colleague's complaint. Without fixing the body, we allow it to go toward health and integration. We touch our innate coherence as a human being, a sense of all-rightness. Life can be chaotic, but we can still experience the underlying sanity of being present in the body in the moment.

Our body is always communicating to others. Our sense of presence communicates. Presence, a sense of being, is the result of a synchronized body and mind. And we can feel this sense of embodied presence in people. We can say, "Ah, that person feels genuine." She is grounded, connected to the Earth, and present in her own deeper sense of body-knowing. She feels trustworthy and available. The theater part of Social Presencing Theater reminds us that we are always enacting and visible to others whether we are conscious of that or not.

Creativity

Resting in not knowing, in open space, is the ground of creativity. The 20-Minute Dance can get us in touch with our creative potential. The practice of nonmanipulation and spontaneity can begin with the 20-Minute Dance. Fresh and genuine gestures arise naturally as we practice letting go of our thoughts, plans, and goals. What often blocks our creativity is the limitation of habit. In Theory U, *downloading* is the word that describes a tendency to project our past habits and experiences onto current reality.[3] Awareness-based change demands that we suspend this barrage of past-oriented thinking and open to the possibility that we can tune in to the emerging future. This attitude of opening to a future that we do not know yet is one definition of creativity.

The experience of naturalness of gesture can also be transferred to creativity in words. My colleague Ricardo Dutra and I have traveled and worked together on multiple projects. He began writing a haiku at the end of each day's 20-Minute Dance so that he had an artifact of the practice. Movement, of course, simply appears and disappears in the space. It comes and goes. However, it leaves an echo, a scent, a feeling that can be captured in a short poem. A haiku is a traditional Japanese three-line poem that celebrates immediate experience. Its form is highly refined; but we can enjoy the spirit of haiku by keeping it simple, by letting three short phrases arise. I also began writing a three-line poem in my journal at the end of the practice. The first line arises from an evocation of the day's 20-Minute Dance. It describes a moment in the practice—something I did. The second line describes a feeling. The third line joins the first line with the second. This third line is often a surprise. You could try it. The 20-Minute Dance provides a spacious environment from which the poem arises by itself, without effort. Here are some of Ricardo's and mine:

Forward and back
Welcoming this moment
Today's healing

Deep exhaustion
Would you care to say something?
Listening

Festive grounds
Of scattered attention
Reunite

Neck and head calling
I'm here, waiting
A secret

Living sadness
Slightly opens a crack
Of brilliance

Can't settle
Falling quickly
Into a laughing sound

The 20-Minute Dance celebrates the body as a sensing organ. In order to deeply understand our organizational or social contexts, we need a good sensing mechanism so we can listen with sensitivity and observe with equanimity. We see with our eyes and hear with our ears, but the feeling-sense, or resonance, from what we see and hear is felt in our entire body-mind system. Sensing is both external and deeply internal. We look out at the world and receive sights, sounds, smells. But the experience of those sights, sounds, and smells is deeply personal and embodied. Although this sensitivity is natural—we are naturally resonant with our experience—the ability to sense can be cultivated and strengthened. Today, more than ever, we need this capacity.

By becoming more and more tuned in to the subtle shifts in feeling that manifest in the body, we cultivate this sensing organ. Our inner condition includes deeply trusting our ability to engage our sense perceptions. By suspending the habitual lenses through which we filter our perceptions, we can see, hear, smell, taste, and touch with freshness and directness. We can experience the world directly. Our wisdom lies in the natural resonance between our inner being and the outer phenomena.

06

THE UNCONCERNED MOMENT
OF MOVEMENT: DUETS

Ma is a Japanese aesthetic principle that translates as a gap, an interval, or the space-time between things. It pervades the traditional Japanese arts—not only the performing arts, such as Noh theater, traditional music, and film—but also calligraphy and architecture. I have attended Noh theater performances in which the actor-dancer moves across the stage, turns, then pauses. In the pause the performer and audience share a heightened moment of beauty. Time stops as the space and the heart open to the fullness of the moment.

I discovered this concept of *ma* when I began studying Japanese court dance and traditional Japanese aesthetics. I love the films of Yasujiro Ozu and Kenji Mizoguchi, particularly the way they linger on images of ordinary people doing almost nothing. The power of this ordinariness and simplicity affects me deeply. Two articles from *Chanoyu Quarterly* (a publication about Japanese tea ceremony) became the basis for my understanding of this profound principle. One is called "*Ma*: A Cultural Paradigm," written by Richard Pilgrim, professor emeritus of Japanese Studies at Syracuse University.[1] The other is a short piece entitled "*Ma*: A 'Usefully Useless' Thing," by Sen Soshitsu XV, head of the Urasenke school of Japanese tea ceremony.[2] Reflections on both of these writings formed the aesthetic basis of my dance work and inform the view and practice of Social Presencing Theater.

The *kanji* (Japanese character) for *ma* is a *torii* gate with the sun shining through. Traditionally a torii is found at the entrance of Shinto shrines and symbolically marks the transition between the mundane and the sacred. The open structure allows the light to shine through. In everyday life, the experience of a gap invites the ever-present qualities of the sun—brilliance, warmth, and clarity—to shine forth and interrupt the speedy crowdedness of our doing and striving.

Although *ma* is a profound spiritual and aesthetic principle, embedded deeply in Japanese tradition and culture, some aspects of this experience are accessible to those of us outside that cultural context. Although the concept of *ma* developed from Buddhist and Shinto thought and is based in a meditative tradition, this feeling-knowing experience touches a human quality in us all. Sensitive to cultural appropriation, we explore the principle and experience of *ma* in Social Presencing Theater with the utmost respect. We recognize that our understanding just touches the surface of this profound experience.

One definition of *ma* by Sen Soshitsu XV is "the unconcerned moment of movement from one step to the next." He is referring to the steps of the tea ceremony, but we can extend this to include the movements made in Social Presencing Theater. The unconcerned moment of movement is the perfect description of the attitude we bring to our gestures—nonmanipulative, without striving. The unconcerned moment of movement is the true move. Sen Soshitsu XV continues, "Yet, unfortunately, most people in the modern world are both unaware of and uninterested in its [*ma*'s] importance. Social pressure encourages keeping busy with all sorts of useful, practical tasks which allow little time for reflection and awareness of the *ma* within and without. The result is widespread restlessness which threatens world peace, and even the existence of life on this planet."[3]

Social Presencing Theater practice emphasizes this gap as a moment of awareness—a direct and immediate experience of the moment in which time and space are not separate. To quote Professor Pilgrim: "The collapse of space and time as two distinct and abstract 'objects' can only take place in a particular mode of experience which 'empties' both the objective and subjective worlds; only in an aesthetic, immediate, relational experience can space be 'perceived as identical with the events or phenomena occurring in it.'"[4]

This may seem like an abstract concept or unattainable realization, but that is not my experience. *Ma* is a celebration of the ordinary moment. It expresses the sacredness in ordinariness. Recently I enjoyed a supper on the porch with a friend. The conversation was lively. At the end of the meal as we sat drinking tea, our conversation fell quiet. Neither of us spoke. We sat in the near dark. The candle flame danced about with the breeze. The symphony of crickets and katydids became vividly present. The moment was completely ordinary, and yet it was, as Professor Pilgrim described, "aesthetic, immediate, and relational."

Perhaps we could spend a moment with these three words: aesthetic, immediate, and relational.

Again quoting Professor Pilgrim, "*Ma* does not exist, or at least does not function, without a certain level of experiential sensitivity—one which is both religious and aesthetic."[5] In our work, aesthetic sensitivity reveals the beauty of each moment. It may not be beauty in a conventional sense, but it is the beauty of genuine feeling. The Greek root of the word aesthetic means "relating to perception by the senses." If we look at the word *anaesthetic*, which means "without feeling or perception," we realize that with perception comes a feeling sense. When we see a tree or hear a voice outside our window, we perceive it in our body-mind system with an immediacy that produces a feeling. That feeling is aesthetic in that it holds appreciation for the beauty of that moment of life.

We are going along with some kind of continuity and then suddenly there is a gap—an interruption in the habitual flow. It is a moment of open awareness. It is a drop of vastness, if that makes any sense—a moment that invites us to *presence* an emerging future, which can simply be an openness to what comes next. We are not blurring or closing down our experience with concepts. Awareness is in the *ma*, and this space is the basis of creativity. In Zen, the space of no mind is the ultimate ground of artistic creativity. In my own training in Dharma Art, true gestures arise from the immediate moment of nowness.

Open space is inseparable from its content. The content is relational. When we look out at or walk through a field, we experience both the open sky and land as well as the crops planted there or animals that graze there. Likewise, we experience both the openness of the social field and the relationships of all the beings who make up the social field. These two aspects—the immediate open moment and the relational quality of all those co-creating the social field are both living in our experience. The kanji for human being, *ningen*, is made up of the kanji for person and the kanji for *ma*. It indicates that to be a human being is to be in relationship to others. Relationship and openness are co-emergent in this moment of *ma*.

Although the concept of *ma* permeates all of Social Presencing Theater as the open present moment from which movement arises, we explore this principle specifically in the Duet practice. These nonverbal conversations foreground the experience of ma. The practice brings sensitivity to the aesthetic, immediate, and relational living in each moment.

Figure 16: Duet sculpture made by students of Moema Cruz, 2017, Recife, Brazil.

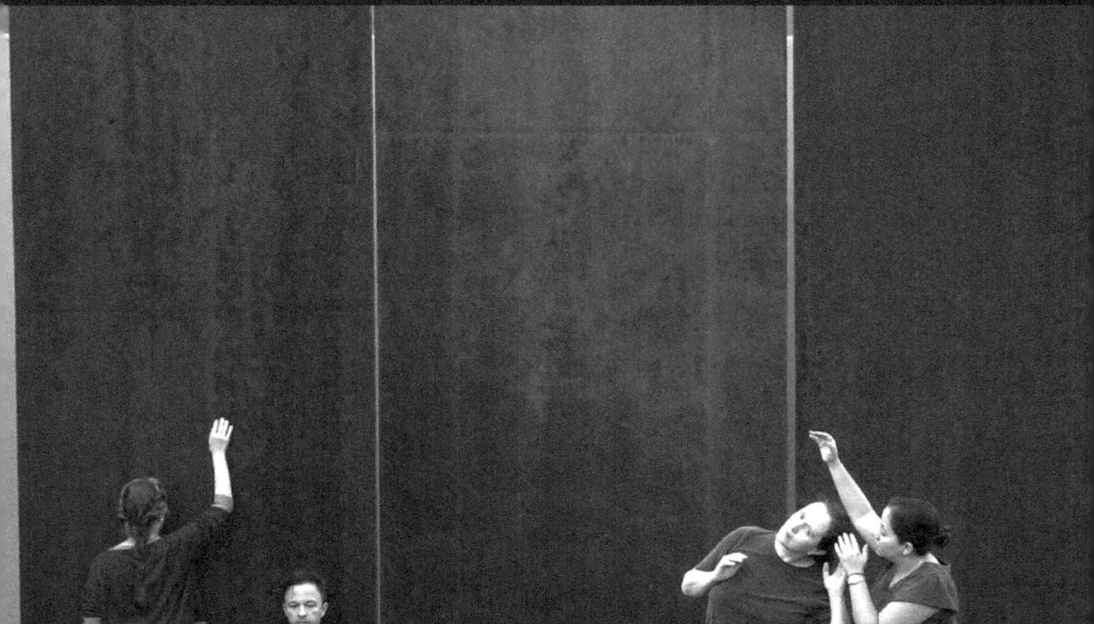

Practice and Reflection Instructions

Stand together with a partner, attending to what is about to happen—to what has not happened yet. First person, begin from a still, standing shape. Without thinking about what to do, without planning, offer a "movement phrase" or gesture. At the end of the movement, pause in a still shape. Hold or rest in this body posture (five to ten seconds). The partner receives the movement phrase or gesture without immediately responding in movement. Both then rest in the stillness, the gap, the ma.

After resting in the space for a few moments, the second person lets a movement arise. The gesture is not a reaction to what was offered by the first person but arises freshly from the shared moment of spacious stillness. (This is not like ping pong, where players try to keep the ball moving back and forth.) Deliberately include the open space where no action is happening. Let movement simply arise naturally, without contrivance, from the shared open space of *ma*. At the completion of the gesture, the second person holds the ending shape. Remain still.

Then the first person allows a movement phrase (gesture) to arise. At the completion of the movement, pause. *Ma*. Then the second person moves.

Continue like this. After a time, when the sense of space is prominent in awareness, you can begin to move together, not forgetting that your gestures arise from the open space of *ma*.

In the Duet practice, we invite a pause as the empty space-time gap between gestures. This pause makes room for the quality of feeling created by the gesture.

The first person offers a gesture. The partner notices what the movement phrase looks like—for example, I see my partner take a step forward and stretch out his arms to the sides. This small phrase of movement communicates a quality that both he and I feel.

The shared resonance of the gesture lives in the open space of *ma*. It is not crowded or rushed. It makes no demand. The space is empty of expectation. I experience this as a sense of fullness free of inadequacy. I do not respond impulsively to what is offered. I am not trying to make a connection because relatedness is naturally present in the space. The gap in time and space enables a deep knowing to shine.

The pause provides a space in which the relationship between my partner and me can deepen. The shared space is full of genuineness and vulnerability. Our attention is on the feeling in the empty space of possibility. The felt sense, even though it may be difficult or impossible to put into words, is vividly present. From that knowing, I make my gesture. My response is not preplanned but arises spontaneously from the experience of my body, the open spaciousness, and a deep sense of relationship. There is very little "me" in the process. And I do not focus particularly on "the other." The expression arises from the genuineness of the moment.

Although we most easily experience the moment of heightened awareness when we are still, the sense of spaciousness can remain as we move. We attend to the arising and continuing movement. Movement can trigger interpretation, story, projection, analysis, and meaning that solidify its ephemeral and nonabiding nature. In this practice we can relax and let go. The *ma* draws our attention to impermanence and the fleeting quality of experience. We can celebrate the unique expression of ourselves and of each person, inseparable from and co-emergent with the vast space of open awareness—the essence of every being and the ground of creativity.

In chapter two I mentioned the four types of listening: confirming, factual, empathic, and generative. These correspond to four types of conversation: polite, debate, dialogue, and generative.[6] The *ma* is at the heart of listening and of conversations that give birth to fresh ideas. Training the body in the nonverbal Duet practice informs how we listen and converse in our everyday work and life. Jiddu Krishnamurti wrote a beautiful piece on listening that describes *ma*:

I hope that you will listen, but not with the memory of what you already know; and this is very difficult to do. You listen to something, and your mind immediately reacts with its knowledge, its conclusions, its opinions, its past memories. It listens, inquiring for a future understanding.

Just observe yourself, how you are listening, and you will see that this is what is taking place. Either you are listening with a conclusion, with knowledge, with certain memories, experiences, or you want an answer, and you are impatient. You want to know what it is all about, what life is all about, the extraordinary complexity of life. You are not actually listening at all.

You can only listen when the mind is quiet, when the mind doesn't react immediately, when there is an interval between your reaction and what is being said. Then, in that interval there is a quietness, there is a silence in which alone there is a comprehension which is not intellectual understanding.

If there is a gap between what is said and your own reaction to what is said, in that interval, whether you prolong it indefinitely, for a long period or for a few seconds—in that interval, if you observe, there comes clarity. It is the interval that is the new brain. The immediate reaction is the old brain, and the old brain functions in its own traditional, accepted, reactionary, animalistic sense.

When there is an abeyance of that, when the reaction is suspended, when there is an interval, then you will find that the new brain acts, and it is only the new brain that can understand, not the old brain.[7]

07

THE SOCIAL BODY:
THE DANCE OF FIVES

Throughout our journey into Social Presencing Theater we return to three areas of attention: body, felt relationships with others, and awareness. Body refers to both our physical body and the social body. A social body is a physical grouping of people. Within Social Presencing Theater, the social body is the group with whom we are practicing; and by practicing we extend that sense of the social body beyond the practice arena. We begin to take great interest in the social bodies with which we engage every day—family or teams at work. We notice our temporary social bodies—those riding in the same subway car or gathered at a Starbucks. We sense that we are always connected to others. We can feel that together we form, for a short time and quite by coincidence, a social body. We become conscious of how we are part of these social configurations.

The second area of attention is our felt relationships with others. As individuals, we feel sensations, perceptions, emotions—the invisible interiority of ourselves. Likewise, social bodies have a felt quality, an interior relational quality that we call a social field. We explore the social field more fully in chapter nine. The third area, awareness, is the open knowing inherent in individuals and groups. Because Social Presencing Theater is a physical, embodied practice, attention is given in this chapter to the social body—the physical presence of people and how they arrange themselves in the space. With the arrival of the Covid-19 pandemic, we worked to heighten our capacity to feel socially embodied even when we practice physical distancing and inhabit virtual social bodies.

Our presence and actions, both subtly and not so subtly, influence others, and theirs influence us. The Dance of Fives increases our ability to sense ourselves as part of ever-present and ever-changing social bodies. The first step is to sharpen our perception of the social body and recognize our part in the inexorable process of physically co-creating social systems. In Social Presencing Theater training programs, we engage in this preliminary embodied awareness practice before the more specific applications of Stuck and 4-D Mapping.

Here we return again to the three bodies—the individual body, the Earth body, and the social body. In the 20-Minute Dance, our attention is turned inward. We attend to our bodies with friendly interest and without judgment. We let our body connect with the Earth body. Becoming more grounded and present reduces the stress and worry that repeat "What about me? How am I doing?" We feel less need for armor. We can relax a little and feel our natural openness and interest in the world around us. The Dance of Fives invites us to let our awareness expand outward with equanimity toward our social bodies. We engage with a small group to heighten our awareness of the social body and the relationships created by the physical-spatial choices we make.

The Dance of Fives is an ensemble activity, a moving arrangement. Participants take notice of what they do, where they do it, and when they do it. We also inquire into why we do what we do. What motivates us? Our actions and nonactions arise from awareness of both what we see out there and what we feel in here. The Dance of Fives enhances our sense of the social body (what we see and do) and its relationship to the social field (the feeling quality of relationships).

In the early 1970s I was asked to teach a movement-improvisation course at the Boston Museum of Fine Arts School. Since I had no idea how to do this, the course consisted of students dancing around freestyle, doing pretty much whatever they felt like doing. I liked working with people who were not trained dancers, whose movements were ordinary rather than stylized, even though most did not have the physical presence or spatial awareness that someone trained in dance might have. As a teacher, my questions were: one, how to encourage more embodied presence in people who were not trained in dance; and two, how to teach the students to shift from individual self-expression to collective creativity as they improvised.

A friend suggested that if I could articulate what the basic elements of this process of movement improvisation were, then that process could be taught to others. That suggestion prompted an investigation into how our actions are connected to the way we pay attention. Since I was interested in improvisation as a performance form, the quality of the work needed to be high. I discovered that the quality of the performance did not depend on the skills, cleverness, or attractiveness of the performers, but did depend on their level of awareness of the whole social body—how clearly they noticed details of movement and spatial design and how willing they were to tune in to and support what was emerging from the whole. A practice form called The Village (see chapter nine) and the simpler version, Dance of Fives, developed from these early questions about how to engage in a co-creative process as a social body.

Practice and Reflection Instructions

Gather in a group of five—a small team or social body. Pay attention to the whole social body as you engage in five ordinary everyday actions: standing, sitting, lying down, walking forward, and turning from facing one direction to another. Limit your movements to only these five ordinary actions, applying mindfulness of body in performing them as you did in the 20-Minute Dance. You can do them in any order, at any time, at any speed. Do not add arms or any stylized gestures. Simplicity supports awareness.

After establishing some mindfulness of the body, let your awareness expand to experience the social body. Attend to the shifting arrangements of people who constitute the social body. Notice proximity (close and far), level (higher than and lower than), and direction (facing toward, away, in, out). When thoughts appear, let them go. Without thinking or planning, let the sense of the social body guide you. Move or pause, sensing into what is emerging. There is no particular goal or anything to accomplish. Simply notice subtle shifts in experience as you move with others in the space. Practice like this for about ten minutes.

Then reflect together on what you noticed. One by one, share something you noticed and then move into open conversation. Begin by simply recollecting and describing: What did I see? What did I feel? What did I do? How did I contribute to what was co-created? Then shift from I to we: What did we co-create? What patterns emerged? What was the feeling tone?

Discovering Patterns

Often in Social Presencing Theater workshops participants are meeting one another for the first time. But we
notice that, within a few minutes of beginning the practice, using just these few movement possibilities, the
groups usually find, without words, some kind of shared
value that enables them to attend to one another and to
co-create an experience of social reality. Often they share,
without speaking about it, a sense of what a "good" team
"should" be and do. In the reflection conversation after
the practice, the team members share their experiences
of the social body, the quality of relationship, and the
process of social field creation. They then have an opportunity to journal about how this experience informs or
relates to their everyday work or life situations.

In accounts of the experiences and insights of Social
Presencing Theater practitioners over the years, we have
noticed repeating social patterns enacted in the Dance
of Fives. Below are reflections from four teams (A, B, C,
and D) that practiced the Dance of Fives. I have chosen
to highlight five patterns of social behavior here, but
there are certainly many more. The patterns repeat so
frequently that they seem like social system archetypes.
Reflecting on behavior patterns reveals how directly our
choices affect others and how the choices of others affect
us. We notice our blind spots—assumptions we make and
then project onto the group. Insights arise that enable us
to better understand the process of co-creating healthy
and creative social systems. You are invited to notice if
these patterns are familiar in your own teams, and to
reflect on additional themes or patterns that arise in the
social bodies in which you live and work.

Pattern One: Opening to the Next Moment

Team A began by engaging in very little movement. The group members seemed to wander around. A participant said, "I could tell I was closing down and retreating into myself. I was confused about what I was supposed to do, worrying about whether I was fitting in. I moved to the edge of the space and sat down. I tuned out. Then someone in the group walked in my direction and sat down next to me. We sat side by side together for a while. I don't even know who was sitting there, but I felt seen and included. I looked up and saw three others standing with an empty space between two of them. I felt that the space was waiting for me to go there and fill it. I got up and joined the others. My attention shifted from thinking about myself to noticing the group and finding my place there."

The pattern of opening to the next moment pattern reveals an important capacity in co-creating teams. Becoming aware of the experience of closing down, disconnecting from what is happening, and going inside oneself is a strong leverage point. It is a reminder that we have a choice. We can continue to feel isolated, or we can open up to the next moment. We do not dwell on the feeling of disconnection by building a story around *why* we feel this. In this account we see how this practitioner's awareness shifted from herself (ego-orientation) to the social body and its ongoing co-creative process (ecosystem awareness).

Pattern Two: Connection and Inclusion

The participant in Team A reported, "Then someone in the group walked in my direction and sat down next to me." In Social Presencing Theater practice (and in life) we can make a choice to attend to someone on the periphery, someone who is falling away from the group. First, we need to see the person. Being aware is already an act of inclusion. In this case, the person who chose to sit next to the Team A participant communicated to her that she was connected, part of the group. The movement was not invasive or demanding. One person's choice opened a pathway for another to join more actively in the practice.

The social pattern of connection and inclusion is a binding factor in our social body that begins with awareness. Open awareness is the basis for feeling connected and included. We notice the inherent connection that is present in the social body. Connection is a given. Everyone on the planet is connected, although sometimes we don't feel like it. Sometimes we make choices, consciously or unconsciously, that exclude ourselves or others. Connection and inclusion communicates a longing to connect with others and for everyone to have a place.

Pattern Three: Social Skin

One Team B participant said, "Our team was beginning to feel harmonious, and then Phil started to walk away from the rest of us and went too far away from the group. What he did made me really anxious, but I didn't know how to get him to come back. We did not know if he was still in our group or not. I felt I had to follow him and somehow make sure he came back. When we talked about it, we all felt confused by what he did."

Often groups have an invisible boundary and a tacit sense of what "too far" means. They create an imaginary social skin that defines and binds their social body. The skin defines what is us and what is outside. If that social skin is rigid, it will not stretch to include the person who moves away from the others; so in this case, the group felt Phil's departure. This team had chosen movements that kept them in close proximity to one another and within their invisible, yet somehow agreed upon, borders. When one person went beyond the imaginary boundary, the others felt concerned that he was no longer one of them.

The social skin did not stretch to include him.

Teams often have one or more persons we call shepherds. They try to ensure that everyone stays in the fold, and they feel concern if they perceive someone wandering too far from the others. Team B also reported a second moment of discomfort when a woman from another team came too close. They said, "She was not one of us." Team B felt their space was invaded, which caused stress. The social skin pattern reflects the value people hold in knowing what is "us" and how a place or space can define identity.

In the reflection, the team talked about the difference between caring about each team member and wanting to control others. They reflected on similar patterns in their work teams and in their responses to unexpected situations. The invisible spatial boundaries were symbolic of the many ways that groups create tacit boundaries that define who is in and who is out. The team appreciated having a boundary (social skin) but experienced how it both excluded others from entering and limited the team members from exploring or allowing a larger perspective. A closely knit social skin with fixed boundaries and inward focus is an archetypal social system pattern. Does this pattern show up in any team, department, or organization you are a part of?

Pattern Four: Social Sameness

In this practice, spatial proximity can define a group (as in the social skin pattern), and so can social sameness. Team C placed a high value on belonging and harmony. In their reflections, they said that they liked their group because it felt harmonious and balanced. When asked what kinds of activities or spatial choices they had made to create harmony, they said, "Nobody stood out as a leader, we were all taking our cues from each other and contributing movements that fit with the others. There was a flow. We ended with everyone sitting in a circle, close enough to be touching, and we could see everyone." They felt like a social body when they were all at the same level, equidistantly spaced, all facing into the center of a circle so they could see one another. They valued the pattern of social sameness as an ingredient in the creation of harmony.

This group reflected on preferences—they valued feeling peaceful. They wondered when harmony is the basis of a creative team and when it is a denial of important differences. They spoke of the forming-storming-norming-performing model of group development[1], and about how in the initial coming together, sameness communicated fitting in and being a good team player. But they also noted that a lack of diversity might have been more comfortable for them, but was ultimately stifling. Could the team direct attention and energy toward harmony and also honestly include difference?

Pattern Five: Loose Distribution

Team D felt satisfied with a loose sense of organization. After completing the practice, they shared that they were aware of one another, or sometimes not. The connection between the members' movements was less obvious. They felt connected through a general sense of awareness. "We had a lot of variety in our group. When Maria wandered away, I still feel that the social body was intact because we were aware of her." They did not need spatial closeness or sameness to feel a sense of social body cohesion. They valued independence, spaciousness, and autonomy. They had no interest in touching one another—in fact, the thought did not occur to any of them. One moved at a much quicker pace than the others. One spent a long time standing and looking out the window. "We each did our own thing, but we didn't lose track of one another. That worked for me," said one practitioner.

One person from Team D said, "At times everyone was so far apart that I lost a sense of connections. I liked that I could do my own thing, but I couldn't feel that we were much of a group." The social skin of this group was so porous that members could wander away. Folks from other groups could wander in and be included. This team valued the individuality of each person. This pattern of loose distribution, with unclear boundaries, is also an archetypal social pattern. Are you engaged in groups in which individuals have a high degree of autonomy? Is there an adequate sense of social container in these groups to feel coherence and potential?

By engaging in co-creating a social reality with small teams, we become conscious of what we are doing in our daily lives, often unconsciously. We become aware that we are creating small societies in our work and life situations every day. We begin to notice that these social bodies are their own entities with their habitual patterns, rhythms, and potential that are different from and greater than the individuals in them. The Dance of Fives calls our attention to the physical embodied aspect of social reality and to our part in creating it.

My friend Georg Senorer told me a story about bringing the Dance of Fives to the board of a bank in Italy. He told me that they were a little skeptical, but they trusted him and engaged in a step-by-step process that began with first attending to their own bodies, then expanding to the space, moving around in the space, and then including the others. The bankers realized they were part of a larger organism. They learned that to some extent they could decide what part to play. However, they also noted that when they felt their power was limited, they needed to be alert and open. Georg said, "The bankers loved this exercise and wanted to repeat it at the start of every meeting. I remember that, thanks to this exercise, the president, a very intelligent man, realized how his very way of communicating interrupted the flow of the dialogue in the group, and he changed it immediately. So the whole team found a new way to communicate."

Laura Pastorini used the Dance of Fives to make visible different patterns of leadership and to encourage creativity and collaboration in a Chilean organization that supports engineers. The forty employees were arranged randomly in groups of five to engage in the practice. Then each group created short narrative presentations about their discoveries in the practice and shared these with the whole group. Laura reported, "The effect of this practice was a strong integration and sense of belonging. Many of the more invisible employees turned out to be very creative or skilled in performing. This practice allowed people in the company who hardly knew one other to engage together to generate an atmosphere of inclusion, equality, and openness."

This practice makes visible the deeper patterns of structure and thought in groups. It can be used as a light diagnostic of team dynamics. Once, some years ago, I saw a group end their practice with the male leader standing in the center and four women sitting or kneeling on the periphery. In the after-practice reflection, the women said that they had not noticed making this choice. But they had inadvertently illuminated an unconscious pattern that did not serve them well in creating their organizational culture. By simply enacting this pattern and seeing it clearly, the team gained insights into how to begin making the necessary changes in a powerful yet nonaggressive way. The practice is a moving snapshot of how groups co-create social reality, making visible how the choices people make can create or destroy collective coherence. Once the system (the actors in a system) can sense the whole, then the change process has already begun.

08

WHAT WE SEE, SENSE, AND DO

What we see, what we sense, and what we do continuously interweave and dance with one another. We see, for example, someone walking toward us. Without thinking about it and frequently without it even registering in our consciousness, we have a felt sense of what we see. This can be subtle—perhaps a slight opening up or closing down. However, our sensing can motivate an action, such as stepping forward or looking down. And this action creates a feeling in those who see it. Everything we do is communicative, often in ways we are unaware of, and we constantly make meaning from what we experience.

The Dance of Fives invites us to investigate this process of seeing-sensing-doing, to increase our sensitivity to the ways in which we engage with our social bodies. The practice heightens awareness of the weaving together of these three nonverbal experiences and invites reflection on subtle patterns. The five social patterns described in chapter seven show the seeing-sensing-doing relationship. Since this connection is so fundamental to all of Social Presencing Theater practice, I would like to investigate these elements of nonverbal communication in this chapter.

This investigation not only brings clarity to nonverbal work, but also sheds light on how we communicate verbally. The seeing-sensing-doing pattern is similar to listening-sensing-speaking in verbal conversations. We listen to others in order to understand the facts. In movement, this can be equated with seeing what people are doing, seeing the physical arrangements of bodies. Besides listening to facts, we also sense a quality or emotion in the speaker's tone. Likewise, in performing and witnessing movement, we sense that the movement communicates a feeling or texture. Doing or performing an action is like speaking. So this process of first listening or seeing with an open mind, then allowing space to sense more deeply into the felt meaning of what is said or seen, and finally responding by speaking or acting describes both verbal and nonverbal communication.

Several Social Presencing Theater practices include speaking, and in all practices the group reflections and dialogues are a vital part of the learning process. I have in the past experienced a jarring disconnect when a spacious and deep movement practice is followed by speedy and discursive speech. I have seen facilitators interrupt the resonant silence created by the practice with their questions and comments. We can, through nonverbal practices, better know our listening and speech patterns. We trust more and more the moments of silence and the world we know through our sense perceptions. By attending to the sensory details of what we see and hear, we gain clarity about how to co-create healthy social relations.

Seeing the Physical Structure
and Spatial Patterns

The Dance of Fives invites participants to notice the movement choices they and others make, the spatial patterns they create, and how those visible social structures hold meaning, feeling, and creative potential. The first step is simply seeing the social body clearly with an open, curious mind. We train ourselves to be careful observers of what is happening physically and spatially. We attend to our own activities, and we attend with equal interest to what others are doing. What is the visible structure that is being co-created as we move about in the space? We notice without judgment or opinion. As we practice the Dance of Fives, we increase our ability to see the physical shapes, movements, and patterns that the group is enacting. We see a social body and the continuously shifting relationships of the parts.

Athletes engaged in team sports develop a sense of the whole playing field or the whole court. They cannot focus solely on the goal posts or the basket in front of them. They attend to the players who are close to them, to those guarding or blocking, and also to the rest of the playing area. They develop a capacity to know not only who is approaching them from the side and who is behind them; they develop an uncanny sense of how fast those people are moving and in what direction. They clearly perceive where support is coming from and where an obstacle exists. An improvising dance troupe is not competing to win a game, but like a sports team, its members need to develop a physical and spatial intelligence that sees the whole with all its moving parts, even when the eyes do not.

Although those of us using Social Presencing Theater in organizations and social projects do not need to develop the capacity of an athlete or a dancer, it is useful to notice how we and others use space. A 360-degree embodied presence (with a good sense of back, what is behind us) enables full awareness of our surroundings. Lacking a preordained outcome or goal, the purpose of the Dance of Fives is to notice that what we do holds information about social field creation. To sharpen our perceptions, the practice instructions invite us to notice three elements—level, proximity, and direction. These are basic ingredients in Social Presencing Theater practices. The choices made around level, proximity, and direction enable relationships among people to form, change, dissolve, and re-form into a continuous unfolding of social patterns.

Seeing levels

In the Dance of Fives, one can choose to sit, stand, or lie down. The three levels represent three different ways of being in the space with others. Each choice conveys a feeling of being higher than, lower than, or on the same level as someone else. For example, we might notice that some are sitting, which inclines us to do the same. Near us, some are standing. We are lower than they are and higher than those lying down. We notice the physical architecture created by our bodies. We can think of being part of a landscape, choosing to be a tree, a rock, or earth. We notice the choices that we and others make without forming opinions or ideas about these choices. We are simply interested in the shifting landscape.

Seeing proximity and distance

We notice how close we are to others or how far apart we are. Again, the emphasis here is on noticing without projecting meaning onto what we see. For example, we might notice density—everyone staying close together in a clump. We might notice a line forming or that one person has moved to the edge of the space. Some activities attract joiners; some don't. Part of the space is empty. We take an interest in these spatial arrangements as they appear and then change.

Seeing direction

We notice the direction we and others choose to face. For example, we notice if we are facing into the group, away from the group, or toward just one person. Knowing what is in front of us, with a clear sense of what is in the space on each side and at our back, clarifies our place in the social body and informs us about others. Noticing the continuously changing physical arrangement of bodies in space leads to the next layer of experience.

Sensing Relational Space

What we see invokes a feeling. I am not referring to feeling as an emotional response (e.g., anger); nor am I referring specifically to a physical sensation (e.g., cold). Although there are elements of emotion and sensation in our experience, I am using the words sensing and feeling to point to a more environmental knowing—a more subtle layer of awareness. Sensing is an embodied knowing of experience through our sense perceptions. In this case, we notice the relationship between what we see and what we sense and how this motivates movement.

The practice invites us to notice a subtle felt resonance between ourselves and others. Something slightly under the surface of our consciousness is present. For instance, a person might say, "When I saw Sam turn to face away from the others, I felt strange." Or, "I saw two people sitting together and something drew me toward them." We boycott the habit of making an instant judgment. We suspend the habit of instantly interpreting our experience. The feeling can be vivid or vague, but it has a resonance—a trueness that reverberates in us and is trustworthy. It informs what we do next.

Sensing levels

By deepening our ability to sense the subtleties of our experience of social space, we notice how the social body feels when, for instance, one person is standing and the others are sitting. One sitter might feel protected by the stander; another might feel threatened. When everyone is sitting together, one person might feel harmony and another might feel uncomfortably conforming. The practice gives us an opportunity to notice our and others' responses to simple shifts in the spatial arrangement of the social body. You may wonder why this is important or how what we notice in the practice informs choices in life.

Last year I had to see a specialist at the hospital. I went there with a friend. We sat in chairs in a hallway, waiting to see the doctor. When the doctor arrived, we stood. She motioned for us to sit down. She remained standing, relatively close to us while we were sitting. The doctor, a person of authority, was standing over us. The feeling of being smaller, not able to meet the doctor at the same physical level, created a sense that we were not equal partners in addressing the issue. In the Dance of Fives, level difference can open conversations about hierarchy, authority, colonization, and power imbalance.

Sensing proximity and distance

During a pandemic such as Covid-19, proximity and distance are major themes. Much of our contact with others must take place at a distance or virtually. We feel the effects of physical distance from family and friends. Although we are grateful to be able to communicate virtually, many of us struggle to feel our social bodies and long for simple physical contact. When we can practice in person with others, we sense closeness and distance. A sense of intimacy, relaxation, claustrophobia, or worry can arise. Every experience is worth our attention. Each has its own integrity and message.

Those of us who work in different cultures pay particular attention to how people physically inhabit the space. Katrin Kaeufer once told me that when she first came to the United States from Germany, she felt that Americans came too close in social situations. Twenty years later, when she attended a social gathering in Germany, she noticed that people were backing away from her in conversations. She had lost her German sense of social distance.

Sometimes at conferences and forums, we have no open floor space and need to do Social Presencing Theater in chairs at tables. Once I was giving instructions on how to do the Duet practice in a conference setting. I was sitting next to a woman from Jakarta, and I asked her if she could help me with a short demonstration: I would make a gesture, then there would be a brief pause, and then she could make a gesture arising from the space between us. We would continue back and forth like that for a minute. She was pleased to try that. I started by making a simple arm gesture—a circle in the air ending with my hand resting on the table. She continued by picking up my hand and stroking her cheek with my hand. This was a gesture that was out of my cultural context—a kind of intimacy and touch that, in my experience, would have been a highly unusual gesture for an American to make in this context. And yet for her, this gesture offered to a complete stranger was natural and easeful.

Most of us have a sense of personal space, an invisible boundary that determines the "right" distance between ourselves and others. In his book *The Hidden Dimension*, anthropologist Edward Hall explains his theory of proxemics and how the use of space is shaped by cultural patterns.[1] The boundaries differ with family members, strangers, people toward whom we have prejudice—

people who are "not like us." These could be folks of a different color, ethnicity, economic status, age, gender, sexual orientation, or mental capacity. We become sensitive to the fact that others might have a very different sense of proximity than we do.

Sensing direction

Standing side by side with another person, we might experience traveling together. Facing to the center and looking out at the edge of the space produce very different feeling senses. Here's an example from the Dance of Fives. The group of five had gathered close together. Then one person changed his direction and turned to look away from the group. Here were the five responses: 1) When he turned away, I felt insulted. 2) When he turned, I could tell he felt isolated. 3) I was glad for the change and curious what would happen next. 4) When he turned away, I noticed there was more room to breathe. 5) The person who turned said, "When I turned away I felt confident that I could go forward and that the team was there to support me." The shift in direction elicited five very different interpretations. The practice shows us how quickly we solidify meaning, and it helps us build capacity to pause, suspend meaning, and simply sense the felt quality of the experience.

Doing: Making the True Move

Actions are what the body does. We could say that the body does only two things: it makes still shapes and it moves. Still shapes can be resting, waiting, intensifying, hanging out. They create stillness in a social space. They can be big or small, balanced or perched. Movements can go up and down, forward and backward. Part of the body can be moving while another part is still. The body has a vocabulary. The dictionary definition of *vocabulary* is "the body of words used in a particular language." The physical body, of course, does not express itself in words. Its language is the felt experience of movements and shapes. Every movement and shape communicates.

In our everyday life we make choices about level, proximity, and direction—where to sit, how close to stand to someone, whether to keep looking at the screen or turn in another direction. I once sat on the board of an arts organization. In meetings, I noticed that when one member spoke who often expressed a dissenting view, others would look down and even turn their bodies away from him. We often make these kinds of choices quite unconsciously. We forget that we are co-creating social reality with our choices—not just what we say, but also how and where we arrange our bodies in space. We both communicate a message and create an atmosphere with our presence and our movement choices. By becoming aware of our choices and those of the others in our social bodies, we come to know how these choices either support or undermine well-being and innovation in a team.

Simplicity

The Dance of Fives has a limited movement vocabulary. We simplify by engaging in only a few ordinary activities that are accessible to and doable by everyone participating. The vocabulary is: walk forward, stand, turn to face another direction, sit, lie down. We maintain a simple vocabulary for several reasons. First, it brings clarity and precision to our experience. We engage with mindfulness, deepening and refining our embodied presence. We experience a profoundness in these movements that have been performed for as long as there have been people. We perform each ordinary movement as though we have never done it before. In fact, we have never before performed the movement at this particular moment. We perform these activities thoroughly, savoring their simple beauty. I have always loved this Balinese saying: "We have no art. We do everything as beautifully as possible."

The second reason for a simple vocabulary is that few and simple options make the practice accessible, easy to enter. Free-spirited folks waving their arms in personal expressive dance can intimidate and inhibit others for whom even standing up to participate is already a stretch out of their comfort zone. Simple movements that all can do enable everyone to take part. Those who feel that the practice puts a lid on their creative playfulness can relax. Those who feel hesitant can gain confidence as they engage within their learning zone.

The third and most important value of simplifying is that our attention can extend out to the open space. We do not need to focus on ourselves and what we are going to do. Too much variety, expressive arm and facial gestures, and demanding eye contact get in the way of the spacious unfolding of the practice. Limited choices allow us to attend more easily to the whole social body and how the space itself informs the choices we make. The simplicity enables us to shift our focus from a narrow sense of personal expression to a wider attention within the ever-shifting social body. We are training ourselves to notice the fluidity of attention and to continuously let our attention relax and open.

Almost a choice

Doing is a process of making choices; in this practice, though, it is a particular kind of choice making. One Social Presencing Theater practitioner in Denmark once said, "It is almost a choice." This felt like a perfect description, because it can seem as if the space makes the choice, not us. That may sound strange, and it is difficult to describe. But rather than focusing our attention on individuals in the space, our attention is on the sense of space itself—on an expressive openness. We engage with others—moving

Figure 18: Village practice.

toward or away, sitting down in the center, turning. The choice of movement is deliberate yet does not arise from imposing our will or from any kind of strong intention. It is as though wakefulness lives in the space and that is what moves us into our choices.

We move based on awareness of the whole—what we see and what we sense. We suspend our thinking about where to move or what to do next. Even with no plan, the next movement emerges with ease. An empty space between two standing figures calls to us. This configuration looks claustrophobic to me, so I move away. The space feels out of balance, so I move a few inches to the left. Sitting back to back with someone feels right, so I will rest here. The present moment and the space guide me. It is almost a choice.

Place and space

Movement needs space. The Dance of Fives not only teaches us about the creation of social bodies, but also makes us aware of the spaces we inhabit. We become aware of how we experience the room and our placement in the room. Places and spaces are containers for learning and transformation. We become more sensitive to the places we live and work and how we inhabit them. Physical spaces have a big influence on the quality of the social field. People can transform a space; likewise, a space can transform people. When the Presencing Institute faculty offers a program, we take enormous care in choosing the place and arranging the space so that it feels inviting, spacious, and also contained. Within the constraints of our homes and work spaces we always have choices about how to create containers that hold the highest aspirations of our social bodies.

A second aspect of space is less tangible. If we suspend our habits of planning our next move and operating from concepts, then we notice that our movements arise from open space. They arise spontaneously—freshly and without constraint. So, we have two different meanings of space—one literal (the space of a room) and one more subtle (open awareness).

Time and nowness

Our activities take place in space and also in time. Bodies move and are still in relation to time. Time is the conceptual framework that indicates a past and a future. Our activities shape time: every gesture has a beginning, middle, and end. Every meeting, every report, every email, every day, every life has a beginning, middle, and end. Many things happen between the beginning and the end; many things change. In the Dance of Fives the individuals and the collective are not the same at the end of the practice as they were at the beginning. Even when the duration of time is short, the social body transforms over time. It knows much more about itself at the end than it did at the beginning.

Individuals and groups have their own timing. Some people move quickly, some slowly. Some are constantly engaged in activity and rarely rest. Others value inaction. The relationship between moving and pausing communicates a sense of timing. This can be likened to breathing—taking in and letting out. The Theory U process has a clear sense of timing—a period of sensing into a context (inhaling), a still period of retreat and reflection, and then a rapid and creative prototyping process with others (exhaling). We develop sensitivity to group timing and to the pacing of the participants in the group.

In addition to the flow of time, we experience nowness. Our practice encourages us to stay present in this moment of experience. The present moment holds a sense of what came before, and it gives birth to an emerging future. But it is not bound by the past or the future. We honor the past with all its heartbreak and glory. It is possible, however, that this present moment is not fettered by what came before or by what we think is to come. This moment is an open sense of not knowing that enables us to access which way to face and where to put our next step. Two different meanings of time—one sequential (beginning, middle, end) and one more subtle (nowness).

Everyday Social Bodies

When I see the world through my choreographer's lens, the bodies in space create everyday dances. Of course, people are mostly socializing, playing sports, waiting in airports, working on construction sites, relaxing at the beach, doing tasks. Nonetheless, from a choreographer's point of view, each activity and arrangement of people is a dance. Sometimes we engage in solos, sometimes duets, in small and large ensembles. The context is no longer the studio or the theater, but some elements remain.

We move toward each other or away from each other

We move or pause, remaining in a shape

We stand, sit, or lie down

We face away from or toward

We occupy the center or the edge

We gather in circles, clumps, lines,

or seemingly random patterns

We join, imitate, follow, or enrich what others do

We take solo space

We initiate, contrast, destroy what others do

Our activity begins, continues, and ends

In everyday life, we continually arrange our bodies in space—sit here, go there. We engage in a spontaneous design process, most of which is unconscious. Choreography, the making of dances, is a conscious design process, composing as people move and pause through space and time. Social Presencing Theater invites us all into this world of becoming aware of the spontaneous choreography of our social bodies in our homes and in public spaces where people gather. We take an immense interest in what people do and the patterns they make while engaging in everyday activities. These patterns create an atmosphere, interpretation, and meaning. Everyday life is a dance that shapes time and space.

09

SOCIAL FIELD: THE VILLAGE

*You start to be aware of perception happening as
it actually does happen from the whole field,
not from within a separated perceiver.*

—Eleanor Rosch, Professor of Psychology
at the University of California, Berkeley

At the beginning of the book I made a distinction
between the terms *social body* and *social field*. The Dance of
Fives highlights aspects of the physical, visible placement
of people to form social bodies. A group of young people
hanging out in front of a school form a social body. We can
see where each one is standing or sitting, what direction
they are facing, and how far from or close to each other
they are. They form a physical structure that is visible to
themselves and to anyone looking at them.

The social field is the quality of the relationships that
make up the social body. Just as we see the social body,

we sense or feel the social field—the interiority of the social body. That interiority is made up of a feeling tone or atmosphere created by the relationships among the people in the social body. The social field is the social relational space. It is invisible yet is felt both by those who co-create this feeling and by someone who might be an outside observer—like looking at the group of young people hanging out in front of the school. The social body communicates a feeling. The tangible social body is a manifestation of the intangible social field. The following passages from Otto Scharmer's books provide further insights into the social field:

> Social field is the sum total of the qualities of relationships we collectively enact. The quality of the relationships gives rise to patterns of thinking, conversing, and organizing that give practical, tangible results. Social field is a system seen from within—the interior of a social system. It is also the social soil—the enabling conditions, the interior conditions that allow healthy plants to grow.[1]

> *Social fields* describe the social system that we collectively enact—for example, the team, the group, the organization, or social system—from the perspective of source. The term "social field" illuminates the interiority of social systems and describes these systems both from the outside (the third-person view) and from within (the first-person view). It investigates the *interior condition* under which social systems shift from one state of interaction to another."[2]

As individuals, our physical body and our inner feeling life are, of course, inseparable. And this is also true of our social bodies and their interiority, the social fields. The physical arrangement of people (visible) is connected to how we sense or feel (invisible). Likewise, choices made from our sense of relationships (invisible) create visible structures. This chapter on the practice called The Village looks in more depth at the sense of the relational space and structure, the social field. The Village invites spontaneous choice making that arises from awareness of the social field. It is a form of movement improvisation that explores ways in which a social system expresses itself.

The Dance of Fives is the basic training where we acquire the tools to attend to and co-create social spaces. The Village is where the social field plays—where we can create the society that we envision. Here we learn what a spontaneously organizing system feels like. A Village can include any number of people. Groups of fifteen to twenty-five provide rich learning spaces. It is best to start with the basic vocabulary of ordinary every-day activity, but with awareness, anything is possible. A simple greeting can morph into a comic duet. Images arise of animals, of caravans, of weddings. Neighborhoods, small groups within the whole group, can form and dissolve. Rituals develop. Leaders emerge. First followers appear. Soloists pop up. Games and innovation arise. Chaos occurs. Calm returns.

Anything is possible in a Village, but nothing is manufactured or forced. The quality of relationships and the level of creativity depend entirely on how aware and how caring the villagers are of the whole. The ingredients of level, proximity, and direction are still the building blocks of structure. Within the structure the group engages in spontaneous movement. Expanded awareness enables it to sense itself as a living system that is co-creating itself moment by moment.

The Village might be the oldest ensemble practice in Social Presencing Theater. It arose in the early 1970s, a time when postmodern dance improvisation became a

legitimate art form. From 1972 to 1976, I practiced movement improvisation and created performance work with
a group of friends in Cambridge, Massachusetts. Bringing
a meditative attitude to our work led to simplifying the
movement choices and clarifying the creative process.
We practiced the Village regularly (sometimes literally
for days on end) to strengthen our ensemble rapport and
collective creative process. We were investigating field
shifts thirty years before I heard the words *field shift*.

Much of what I know about the creative force of social
bodies and social fields entered my life with this early
experience of the Village. Over the years I have improvised across disciplines—dance, theater, architecture,
poetics, visual arts—and in diverse styles. Each person
brought his or her own expression. And yet the attention
was always on the collective body—the whole. Each of us
was contributing movement, stillness, words, or images.
But it was the social body that was performing. By sensing
ourselves as a social body, we could allow the performance to unfold as it wanted to. It was not about any one
of us. The more we attended to what wanted to emerge
and the more we let go of directing anything, the more
genuine and powerful the performance became.

*I feel that we're constantly trying to convince the
world that there's beauty in movement. That space is
an eloquent medium. That text is not always necessary.*

— Choreographer Bill T. Jones[3]

Figure 19: Original Village practice group, Cambridge, MA, David Appel, Larry Teitelbaum, Raymond Allen, Tom Krusinski, 1974, Photo credit: Michael Harris.

stay with the prescribed movement vocabulary, without using arm or hand gestures. Use mindfulness in performing the activities and to let your awareness antennae attend to the social field and to the sense of open space. When thoughts arise, let them go. You can always go back to thinking once the Village is over. Choices arise from awareness of the social field and the space. Create social structure by grouping in "neighborhoods" or by picking up, imitating, repeating, or otherwise developing movements and shapes. Follow, join, enrich, enhance, or build on what someone else has offered. Add contrast or initiate something new. If you are an experienced practitioner with skills in the basics, open your movement vocabulary to include anything that can be held within the container of awareness of the whole Village.

How we attend

At the end of the Village practice, the "villagers" reflect on two questions: Did we co-create a village where we would want to live? How did I contribute to creating this village? That is really the point of the practice—understanding the qualities of the village and developing the capacities needed to co-create a village where everyone has a place. The village is a microcosm of the society. Everything we experience in our teams and communities shows up in the village. The practice invites us to experience individually and collectively what contributes to creating healthy villages and what detracts from that. The outcomes rest on how we attend.

The Village experience depends completely on our level of awareness—an ability to notice the details of our unfolding experience and also to maintain a sense of the whole. We see the others moving in the space, and we attend to our own changing physical sensations, thoughts, and emotions. We notice the objects of our awareness, both external and internal, tangible and intangible. And we also have the ability to sense the quality of the space, the atmosphere. An obvious example of this in our work life might be when we walk into a room in which a contentious meeting has just ended. The room is empty, and yet a feeling lingers in the room. We sense it before we think about why this is so, or about what happened there. This sense of atmosphere is invisible, but it is clearly experienced. It is not imaginary or spiritual. Although it is intangible, it is clearly perceptible. This atmosphere of the social field is in our awareness.

The instructions for the Village are to pay attention to the whole. However, our attention moves fluidly. We feel our body rising from sitting to standing; then we engage in a trio with two others close by; then we notice someone across the room, which opens our awareness of the whole space. Our attention shifts from close to far, from inner to outer, from self to others. The Village practice encourages this fluidity, but always beckons our sensing antennae out to the whole space. The way we use our eyes supports this attending to the whole space. We are invited to use a soft gaze. We engage our whole body as a sensing organ, and this often means we need to relax how we use our eyes. I would like to linger for a moment on this topic.

When we feel grounded, and the back of the body is present in our awareness, then our front body, including our eyes, can relax. Without a good sense of the three-dimensionality of the body, we can feel as though the front of our body is plowing into a room and that we are navigating with our eyes. Our eyes are grasping at objects and people. This can be accompanied by a feeling of trying to connect. When we feel the presence of the back body, we can relax, allowing us to "rest in the eyes," as I heard one of my qigong teachers, Richard Reoch, say. We let our eyes soften, loosening our direct focus, and heighten our peripheral vision.

Soft eyes support a sense of spaciousness—openness of mind and openness around the body. We are aware of those beside us, traveling in the same direction that we are. We are aware of those behind us, although we do not actually see them. We are able to let our awareness antennae extend out to include the entire social body. We are both a co-creator of the social body and an observer of details. We notice where there is movement, where stillness. We notice dense spaces and open spaces. We notice what feels inviting and what does not. We notice the patterns the social body creates and their accompanying environmental feelings.

Everyone has a place

This open awareness enables us to notice the diversity of members of the social field and to make choices that are respectful of everyone. People are all so different. Some naturally initiate activity. Some naturally join, support, build on, follow. Some hang back, reluctant to join, while others take the lead. Some move quickly from one activity to the next; some enjoy sitting still. As long as villagers are able to suspend their thinking to attend to the whole with open minds and hearts, the village manifests its sanity and deep caring.

However, the Village practice also affords the opportunity to notice what causes us to close down. We become more aware of our blind spots, both individually and collectively. For example, in a recent Village practice, a woman reflected, "I felt like I was on the school playground as a child. I could not find a way to join." Often small groups arise within the village in which people are highly engaged. They feel connected and creative, and build a strong rapport with one another. This experience can become so seductive that they lose awareness of those outside of their immediate surroundings. They create a social grouping that unintentionally communicates exclusion. By being aware of the whole, care for the whole naturally arises.

The practice is always followed by a reflection and conversation about what we learned. We notice that when we have a rigid idea of what an ideal village should be or what needs to happen, that can cause a feeling of separateness and frustration. We notice when we are dissatisfied with our experience and trying too hard to make something else happen. We notice that we make assumptions and projections about other people's choices. We notice that we are either comfortable or uncomfortable taking solo space. We notice what attracts followers and what does not. We learn about our own place in the village and what makes it possible for every person to feel their place.

The village as a space for creativity

Society-making is a creative act engaged in by every person on the planet. There are no bystanders. Every day each of us co-creates with everyone else on the planet the world in which we live. The Village practice heightens our awareness of this fact. It is a lab for social reality creation. It is a self-organizing and continuously unfolding collaborative process that involves making choices. Making choices can arise from curiosity, care, confidence, and the open space of not knowing. It can also be an expression of fixation, self-absorption, or fear.

Like all Social Presencing Theater practices, the Village has no preordained end goal. Each village creates its own shared values during the process of creation. There is never any instruction to create an ideal village, although participants often speak of well-being as the quality of a good village. Villagers only have the ingredients—the basic activities—and instructions on how to pay attention. That is all they need. There is nothing specific to accomplish. With this attitude, they can see what is emerging moment by moment as they attend to the social field of this particular social body. Creativity arises from presencing, the practice of perceiving so deeply into the collective space of the present moment that we can hear the future, which inexorably arises from the present.

Improvising musicians and dancers are not thinking about what notes to play or what gestures to make next. They are letting those notes and gestures come to them. Great music comes from a space far greater than the sum of the individuals. Nowness is outside of our usual perception of time passing. The past, with all its freedoms and oppressions, and the future both live in nowness. Social Presencing Theater calls upon this spirit of the improvising artists who gesture from the openness of now.

On one level, the practice is about finding our place in an ever-changing environment where things are continuously falling apart. In the village, people are constantly moving and shifting positions. The practice is to remain open to not knowing, to the unexpected, without either manipulating or closing down. We notice what causes us to operate from *ego* self-confirmation and what causes us to operate from *eco* awareness. The social body, like a human body, has multiple parts, and all the diverse parts need to work harmoniously together to maintain well-being. In the body, each part has its own role. The liver does not do the job of the toe. The eye is not interchangeable with the stomach. Likewise, in the social body, each of us has a role to play; and yet, when we operate with awareness of the whole social body, not only is this wholeness meaningful for us personally, but it also guarantees that the team body will move toward its most caring and creative potential.

Relaxing as the key

The Village is an invitation to move from an individual egosystem approach to an ecosystem experience through continuously letting go of self-centralization and relaxing our attention—extending our awareness to include the whole. We notice when our thoughts and emotions shut down our connection and our ability to spontaneously create with others. By noticing, we can immediately let those restrictions go and enter freshly into the next moment.

The key to building a village is to relax without being careless or inattentive. When we bring too much ambition or pressure to connect, we notice that and relax. When we feel confused, we relax. When we are discontented with what is happening, we relax. When we become excited about what a great experience we are having, we relax. My teacher Sakyong Mipham points to a habit all of us share: "always wanting there to be another now." We want a better now, a safer now, a more intense now, a less intense now, a higher now, a deeper now. We judge this moment as deficient according to our standards of what a meaningful experience should be.

In the Village practice, each moment is complete and meaningful. Each moment is an invitation to open up to what is actually happening and to engage with that. Moments when nothing seems to be happening are as valuable as moments when something seems to be happening. We appreciate the spaciousness of boredom. We have no prejudice one way or another. Whatever our experience is of the social field, that is our experience. It is perfect. It is the perfect village for the people who are creating it. It is worthy of our participation and reflection. We attend to it with open interest, a dash of courage, and a pinch of carefreeness.

Social Presencing Theater practitioner Laura Pastorini has invited client teams to do multiple Village practices over a period of time to make visible the evolution of the group. She also uses it to explore patterns of leadership in teams. Laura said this about a client practicing the Village, "They could recognize and manage the different centers of power that appeared in the Village. They were better able to understand the value of bottom-up initiatives and could acknowledge diverse qualities of leadership—collective female leadership and horizontal collaboration—and the role of vulnerability in leadership."

With the Village practice, our awareness is heightened, and in our everyday life we perceive the world more directly. We are less in our own bubble. We are more aware of the space, and the sense of separateness between ourselves and others lessens. We experience social fields in our everyday life when we focus less on ourselves, when we let go of our opinions and agendas

and actually listen and feel. When we relax our awareness and perceive from a place of open mind and heart,
we can easily sense the social field. I often saw our colleague Beth Jandernoa sense deeply into a group and
speak from the collective wisdom of the field. There was
no separation between her awareness and the collective
field awareness.

There are many parts to any system—various people,
values, loyalties, points of view, histories, and stories.
There are many differences, often leading to conflicts,
mistrust, disrespect, and hatred. But what are the deeper
patterns under all the differences and unique qualities? That is one of the questions that Social Presencing
Theater engages. Is there an invisible field of connection
and potential care and creativity? If there is an underlying wholeness (social field, social fabric, field of awareness), how do we create conditions that enable that
wholeness to be expressed without losing the rich diversity of the parts?

Reflection Guidelines

Aside from the movement experience itself, how we
reflect on our experiences in the Village practice and in
all the Social Presencing Theater practices has become
more refined over the years. Social Presencing Theater
practitioners have developed methods to sharpen
first-person observation skills, to give a language to nonverbal experience, to suspend meaning-making, and to
let fresh connections between the Village practice and
the various villages of our everyday life arise. They recognize the importance of differentiating between
first-person description and the meaning we make of
our experience, both individually and collectively. Social
Presencing Theater is an invitation to deepen our felt
experience by being present with the vividness of each

moment. Then we can sense into the voice of the village itself. What is the village saying to us? Different practitioners have developed a variety of ways of reflection on the Village experience, but it generally follows this format.

First, we remain still in our ending body shape and have a minute of silence to let the resonance of the village be present. Then we sit together, sometimes in small groups and sometimes in the whole group, and describe our experience using "I saw," "I felt," "I did." We do not interpret or project what we think. For example, I might say, "I saw several of us making a game of opening and closing a circle." Or "When I saw her lying down with three people standing over her, I felt sorrow." Or "When I saw a line of people running through the space, I joined." We hear each person's description of a particular moment in the village that stood out for them.

Then there is another moment of silence, and we rest in an open awareness of what we have heard. Last, we have an open conversation around themes, patterns, or happenings in the village. The themes are often about the formation of neighborhoods (subgroupings), or inclinations to follow, join, disrupt, enhance something that is present, or initiate something new. Other themes might be the balance between movement and stillness, or the habit of being in the center or on the periphery. We notice what we value—such as clarity or innovation. Then we try to get a sense of the voice of the village. If the village could speak, what would it say? We shift our attention from what we see, sense, or do to what message the village might have for us. Finally, we take time to connect this village experience to our everyday life and work contexts.

An architect said that she was sitting in a small group in the village, enjoying the company of the others. Then she stood up, and a simple insight came to her. She noticed when she stood that she could see the whole configuration of the group she had been sitting with. A clarity arose in her mind that if she were to put a little more distance between herself and her team at work, she might have a better perspective on how to lead. She realized that being very hands-on with her team made it difficult to sense a direction. The insight that arose from her Village experience helped her balance camaraderie with leadership in a more skillful way.

Aesthetic Language Cards

It is difficult to convey the quality of nonverbal experience in words. In order to support the reflection process, Ricardo Dutra and I created a set of cards we call Aesthetic Language Cards. We were interested in finding ways to increase the clarity of perception. We also recognized that people were familiar with and often spoke from a psychological or emotional frame of reference. We were looking for fresh language that drew attention to and expressed the layered patterns in the social field. We felt that an aesthetic language taken from visual design and the movement arts could draw out the felt quality of these patterns.

With participants in the Social Presencing Theater advanced programs, we prototyped and received multiple rounds of feedback on the cards. We designed the cards around a three-tiered structure. The thirty-six cards are divided into Visible Structure (physical manifestation), Relational Structure (sensed experience), and Deep Structure (quality of attention). The cards were prompts that brought fresh thinking and language to the process of reflection.

The twelve Visible Structure cards draw attention to what we see. We think we are observant, but it is remarkable how much we don't notice in our daily contexts. By

Figure 20: Aesthetic Language Cards. Design by Ricardo Dutra.

attending to what is visible in the village, we notice the choices that we and others make simply on a physical-doing level. One card says *Center & Periphery*. Was there more activity in the center or at the edges? Did I prefer one place over another? Another card asks what *Social Structures* appeared. Another card prompts reflection on *Boundaries*, another on *Proximity*. Did I choose to be closer to others or to leave distance between us? We heighten our ability to simply see the shifting visible structures that are created and dissolve throughout the Village practice.

The twelve Relational Structure cards are designed to deepen our ability to co-sense. Our sense of the village, or the feeling quality of it, influences our choices—how we engage and what we engage in. The *Attraction to, Disinterest in*, or *Aversion to* card helps us discern activities and places that are welcoming from those that, for whatever reason, are less engaging. The card reminds us that all three experiences—liking, disliking, and not caring—appear in the village. Our choices create relationships that are our social reality. The cards *Balance* and *Empathy* prompt reflections on where we experience these qualities in this village. The cards deepen our ability to sense and to articulate the feeling tone of experience.

The twelve Deep Structure cards invite us to investigate our awareness—the source from which we operate. Our awareness can be open to not knowing (represented by the *Openness* card) and to what wants to emerge, and it can be limited by *Habitual Behavior*. The *Surprise* and *Not Knowing* cards call our attention to the emerging moment-to-moment experience and how our true moves create the social fabric of open curiosity, deep care, and the courage to be who we are. Although the cards were made for Village reflections, they have added a depth and clarity to other Social Presencing Theater experiences and even to other group processes.

10

THE PERFORMANCE OF
LEADERSHIP: FIELD DANCE

If it comes out of nothingness, whatever you do is natural,
and that is true activity.

—Shunryu Suzuki, in *Zen Mind, Beginner's Mind*

Performance is such an interesting word. Sadly, it is often associated with unpleasantness, anxiety, being judged, or being put on the spot in a negative way. In the performing arts, we are used to distinguishing practice or rehearsing from performance. In the 1970s, I heard the now somewhat hackneyed expression, "Life is not a dress rehearsal." The expression may be trite, but it reminds us that living is performance. Being present and showing up fully in life can be seen as a performance. I do not, of course, mean being artificial or showing off. I am referring to showing up genuinely and fully as who we are—and allowing others to see and experience us.

I learned the performance practice that became the Field Dance in the mid-1970s from Lee Worley, retired chair of the Theater Studies Program at Naropa University and a holder of the teachings on Mudra Theater. She described in her book *Coming from Nothing: The Sacred Art of Acting*. Lee offered the practice called Presenting Yourself to the Audience as a way to cultivate presence and a sense of being.[1] I learned it as a part of my training in making an entrance onto the stage, speaking spontaneously, and exiting the stage. I adapted this form as a three-part movement practice. The emphasis was on awareness of the open space (which included the audience) from which the movement arises.

The first time I offered the Field Dance to a group of executives in Vermont, we did the practice outside in a beautiful grove of trees. It was a practice to encourage space awareness, which drew forth the naturalness and unconditional confidence of the presenter. Two pines created the stage entrance and exit locations. Being in nature encouraged us to raise our gaze and connect with a larger sense of space. Peter Senge began to call the practice the Field Dance, and the name stuck. Gestures arose from the open space of not knowing—from the field. Often the Scotch Highland cows would come to the edge of the pasture and watch us.

Figure 21: Field Dance, Mexico, 2019. Arawana Hayashi.
Photo credit: Victor Rejón.

Practice and Reflection Instructions

Create a setting similar to a stage and audience by placing chairs in a semicircle, preferably facing a blank wall, which serves as a backdrop. The chairs at each end of the semi-circle are closest to the wall, no closer than two meters from it. The area in front of the chairs is the stage. Everyone begins the practice sitting in the chairs, as an audience simply looking at the empty stage in front of them.

1. The person sitting at one end of the semi-circle (the first person) rises and walks to the side of the stage space that is closest to their chair.

2. First person: Walk directly to the center of the space, turn to face the sitters, and stand there.

3. Feel your embodied presence (feet on ground, head to sky, back of the body) and sense the whole space, the social field. Do not focus your attention on individual sitters. Keep eyes soft with presence to the back body. Remain there until you have a sense of the whole social field.

4. Those sitting in chairs: Notice your embodied social experience. Let thoughts go and remain present to the experience.

5. Standing person: Turn and walk with presence to exit the stage on the opposite side from where you entered.

The form is that people alternate sides. The first person enters from one side and then exits to the opposite side. Next person enters from the side where the previous person exited and then proceeds to leave on the opposite side from where they entered. And it goes back and forth like that.

6. Second person: Rise from the chair at the other end of the semi-circle, on the side where the first person has exited. First person: Return to the audience semi-circle and sit in the chair that the second person has just vacated. Second person: Go to the edge of the stage closest to you and repeat the sequence: walk to the center of the stage space, face the audience, attend to that experience, turn, and exit the stage on the opposite side from where you entered. The third person rises when the second person leaves the stage. The second person sits in the vacated seat.

7. The third person repeats the practice, and this continues until all have had the opportunity to be the walking-standing person.

8. When everyone has completed their walking-standing practice, the group members reflect on their experiences as the walking-standing person and as the sitter.

Next, repeat the steps, with each person offering one phrase of movement. The process for entering and exiting is the same: walking from the edge of the stage space into the center, turning to face the sitters, and completing the practice by turning and walking to exit. However, this time when standing in the center, each person offers one phrase of movement that arises from attending to the social field and to the open space of not knowing. The gesture or activity arises spontaneously, without planning. At the end of the movement phrase, it is important to hold the ending shape for a few seconds; then return to standing, pause for several seconds to again sense the field before exiting.

The practice can be developed into multiple movement phrases and can include spoken words as long as the gestures and words arise from the field of openness and are not preplanned or the result of a narrow sense of self-expression. They arise spontaneously from the awareness of the open space of emergence and from the social field. The practice is followed by a group reflection on what each member noticed as a stander or as a sitter.

Letting go and letting come

In the U process, the gesture or action between *sensing* and *presencing* is called letting go. We sense into our surroundings and into ourselves, and then we let go of our thoughts and memories and open up to the present moment. By fully attending to the present moment, presencing, we sense possibility for action—the emerging future. In the Field Dance, we let go of any preplanned idea of what we could do and let come a gesture that arises from that openness.

Naturalness

In our work and community lives, many of us are called upon to stand and perform in front of a group of people seated in front of us. Leaders often find themselves in this position. We can project a myriad of downloaded interpretations onto this familiar social structure from our past experiences. The person in front may be a teacher, a priest, a lecturer, an entertainer, a manager, a politician, a facilitator, or a leader. As a sitter, I am a student, a parishioner, an audience member, a meeting attender, a worker. The person standing seems to be in a position of authority. He or she is higher than I am, literally, standing while I am sitting. Experience tells me that the person standing could be offering or selling information, directions, entertainment, or inspiration. And I, sitting with others, am receiving. In a consumer society it follows that if the person standing is selling, then I am buying. And I am entitled to judge, to evaluate whether I am getting my money's worth, whether the stander's performance is worth my time and attention.

This attitude, prevalent in transactional society, is not conducive to collaborative creativity. The Field Dance invites us to let go of the conventional interpretations of this particular social configuration. It offers us an opportunity to suspend our habitual ways of engaging with the performer-audience relationship and invites us into a co-creative social field. It points our attention to the fact that we are always co-creating social reality with others, and we could shift our involvement in a way that creates a holistic environment rather than a fragmented one. When this happens, the stander's gesture can arise from naturalness, from a lack of self-conscious restriction. The viewers' experience is also natural, arising from a collective sense of genuine curiosity and warmth.

The key, as in all our other practices, is awareness of the whole and a sense of appreciation. We see the goodness in people. Both the stander and the sitters are free of the feeling of separateness and unequal power. They become aware that together they create an open, shared experience of possibility. They can drop the us and them mentality and expand into a sense of collective wholeness.

Spontaneity

Each stander's gesture is a true move arising from open space, from nothing. The gesture is fresh, uncontrived, and powerful. It is not exactly self-expression, although it is unique and personal. It expresses both the vulnerability and the strength of that person. The standers experience themselves in this highly visible situation. They sense the presence of the group and the whole space—the openness of the experience. They do not need to close down their experience by overlaying preconceptions and old memories on it. Whether we are standing in front of a group of sitters, or we are sitting with someone standing in front of us, we do not jump to a conclusion. We can relax, open up, and recognize that our gestures arise from this co-created social openness.

Awkwardness

When we practice the 20-Minute Dance or the Duet, we pause between movements to be with the not knowing.

The movements are spontaneous, based simply on what the present moment feels like. When we are in a group practicing the Field Dance, inevitably, some feel self-conscious or stage fright because the practice is unfamiliar and we are on the spot. The habitual, downloading mind tells us that we are being judged, that we have to protect ourselves in some way—protect ourselves from being seen. When that happens, the instruction is simply to notice that feeling and bring it along with us.

We genuinely do not know what is going to happen or what we are going to do. We enter the space and wait for our movement to arise. There is great value in not knowing. The not knowing can manifest as awkwardness or uncertainty, even panic. We welcome whatever we feel. Nothing has gone wrong. We let it be. We even develop an appetite for this kind of uncertainty. We can experience vast openness in this moment of slight panic. We can feel that the rug of security is being pulled out from under us. And still we can still feel our feet on the ground, a good sense of what is at our back, and we let our sensing antennae extend out to the space. That moment of awkwardness holds immense beauty and power. Awkwardness is genuineness. The value of awkwardness—not knowing what we will do next—is the basis of genuine creativity.

Jo Ha Kyu

The principle of time in all of the traditional Japanese performing arts is called *jo ha kyu*. *Jo* is an "orderly beginning." *Ha* is "breaking," as in a mirror shattering into many pieces. *Kyu* is a "rapid conclusion." This sequence is experienced in the Japanese theater as an almost imperceptible quickening of pace from the beginning to the end. The timing does not build up to a climax and then reach a denouement, as in Western classical music or theater. It begins in an orderly way and then goes in a variety of directions. The end simply is the result of letting go. The end is the natural result of the beginning and the middle. It cannot be controlled or changed. It freely moves forward.

In Japanese Noh theater, no curtain comes down at the end of the performance. The *shite*, the main character, simply exits quickly by way of the *hashigakari*, the upstage bridge. He moves out of the viewers' sight—perhaps to some other realm. At the end of a Gagaku performance the musicians play music as the audience leaves the theater.

The Field Dance form can develop as a series of movement phrases. A beautiful moment in one of the Social Presencing Theater advanced programs was seeing each person offer a three-phrase dance with a three-line poem. Each phrase began with no plan, but we could feel a profound grace in the subtle quickening of pace that happened naturally. Endings were simply an invitation to open further.

Receiving

Performance is an exchange, a process of giving and receiving for both the one offering a gesture and those who witness it. It is a nonverbal conversation, just like the Duet. There is mutual appreciation and positive regard for the basic goodness of each person. The Field Dance form allows for a pause after each person's gesture and before that person exits. Making a gesture is similar to speaking, if we were using words. Frequently, however, the stander gestures and immediately exits without waiting to receive, without listening for a response. The response is not meant to indicate whether people liked or disliked what was offered, and yet that is often the gesturer's reference point. But the practice is not about how to get self-confirmation.

In the pause after we offer our gesture, we are waiting to feel that our gesture was received. If we wait with openness and no sense of expectation, we experience the subtle atmosphere of response. And that response is nourishing. Receiving contributes to personal and collective sustainability. It confirms the deep human connection that we all have with one another. Communication closes the feedback loop of giving and receiving. Gestures themselves disappear into the space, but they leave behind a quality of resonance and knowing. The viewers have had an experience. Every person's gesture in the Field Dance enriches and transforms the social field. We have witnessed this over and over again. The basic goodness of the collective is palpable in the space.

11

ART MAKING AND SOCIAL ART

In visual design, the relationships between the specific parts (shapes, colors, materials) either give rise to or detract from clearly communicating the essential quality of the work. In choreography the movements and the spatial arrangements of the dancers (as well as the costumes, sets, and music) all contribute to creating a coherent whole. When the various parts or components seem to be organized in a satisfying way, we say that a work of art "works." Looking into the design and aesthetic principles of parts and wholes has informed my thinking on how we as social systems can shift from parts (egosystem limitation) to whole (ecosystem awareness).

Social Presencing Theater explores the relationship between the parts (individuals) and the whole (social body) and how this relationship holds both an aesthetic quality as well as meaning that informs the social system's innovation process. We are interested in the choices we make and how those choices create or undermine a sense of coherence of the whole.

One way I have studied the topic of parts and whole is by engaging in a visual design practice that I learned many years ago from Trungpa Rinpoche. The practice is called Object Arranging. We chose three ordinary objects, either human-made or natural, and arranged them on a large sheet of white paper. The idea was to investigate an ancient Asian principle of composition called Heaven, Earth, and Human. The process of perception, art making, and the product made were inseparable.

The Heaven principle connects us with a sense of open space, with vision, and the first inspiration or gesture arises from that openness. This might be an intention. The Earth principle is groundedness. It anchors the initial inspiration and brings it to Earth. The Human principle is what joins Heaven and Earth. The Human principle is the heart.

We each sat in front of a large sheet of white paper with our objects beside us. We were to meditate while resting our attention on the blank white paper. The blank paper was our reference point for the open space of possibility. Then we let our hand reach for the first object—the object that manifested the Heaven principle—open, vast, accommodating. We placed that object on the paper. We were not to think about it or come up with a representation of Heaven—instead, we were instructed to sense what would establish the most open and accommodating environment.

Then we again sat and rested our open attention on the paper and the object.

Then we selected the second object as the Earth principle—the thing that would provide grounding. Again we allowed our hand to be drawn to the object, rather than trying to figure out the right choice. If Heaven expresses openness, possibly vision for what is to be created, then how does that open vision land on Earth? What allows it to go forward? Again, this was done without trying to figure anything out. We were activating our sense perceptions, particularly our visual sense and feeling sense, without the limitation of thinking what it might mean. We were not representing anything or trying for a literal, conventional meaning. Resting with the second object in hand, feeling the whole body and gazing at the paper with soft eyes, we placed the second object on the white paper.

The placement of the second object created a relationship. Communication was present between the objects. Again we sat with the paper and the two objects and let our attention rest on what we saw and what was happening in our own body-mind.

Then we selected our third object—the Human principle. Where on the page would the object join Heaven and Earth to complete the composition? Sometimes the object would be placed literally between the Heaven and Earth objects, but most often the object would find its place somewhere else on the paper. The blank space would call the object to some surprising, fresh, humorous, tender, bold place that the mind could never have thought of. The practice shifted my attention from what I wanted to create, what I wanted to impose on the objects, to finding the natural order of the objects on the paper. Making the choice was not about me imposing my will. I needed to be present and attend to my actions, and I needed to be open to what was wanting to emerge, to the composition that was beyond my opinion of what I liked or did not like.

This process of seeing and sensing into the quality of the object and its potential place, letting go of any idea about where it should be placed, feeling drawn, and then placing the object with confidence is a perfect description of the Social Presencing Theater journey. The sense of being present and then opening mind and heart to what wants to happen is the crux of our work. It is the basis of the creative process. From an open awareness we make a choiceless choice. This is not self-expression, as I understand the word. It is allowing the space of openness to express itself. The space of the white paper, the space of the empty stage manifests as an open, spacious quality of mind. The space expresses itself through gestures in the same way that it does through the placement of objects.

The essence of the composition was directly communicated by the arrangement of the objects. Each person's arrangement had its own unique quality, even when we all had the same objects to work with (coins, shapes, matchsticks). Some were spacious and Zen-like, some were crystal clear, some expressed richness, some were playful, some were highly dynamic. But it was obvious that when the objects were arranged in a particular order the sense of the whole was present and coherent. And when they were arranged in another way, the sense of the whole was confused and lost. It did not depend on the objects. It depended on where they were placed on the page.

When there was a sense of the whole, each object stood out with its own integrity and quality. Each object had its own space to *be*. It was fully and exactly what it was. The sense of the whole was somehow related to each object being in its true place so it could be seen and experienced clearly. We as students could feel when the objects were too close to one another, when they were competing or overshadowing one another, in a power struggle for attention, making demands on one another. Likewise, we could feel when there was too much distance between the objects, so that they seemed to lose one another. The space between them felt thin and without energy.

This experience led me to think about how this practice might be translated to embodiment practice. I created a series of early Art of Making a True Move practices in which three, six, or nine people would arrange themselves in studies of this natural composition of Heaven, Earth, and Human. When we engaged with the sense of space, without preconceived thoughts, we invoked the Heaven principle. The visible structure of the social body was the Earth element—physically grounded. The Human principle was the quality of relationships—the social field—invisible but vividly present. The social sculptures in Stuck, 4-D Mapping, and other practices are compositions, each one holding its own meaning. Object arranging made me more sensitive to the social-spatial compositions in Social Presencing Theater and in my everyday life, and to the possibility that these compositions hold meaning that supports our change efforts.

Prototyping Social Art

Today Social Presencing Theater is practiced by small groups in ordinary work, educational, and community settings; but it did not begin there. When I read *Theory U* in 2007, I thought of Social Presencing Theater as a performance form—a way of recording a transformation process in one part of a system that could be shared to trigger change in other parts of the system. I began trying things out at gatherings hosted by the Shambhala Institute for Authentic Leadership in Halifax, Nova Scotia. I gathered a small team of interested people (including Adam Yukelson, who became the co-designer of u.lab for the Presencing Institute), we interviewed participants, then created a performance for the whole community that was based on the interviews. After the performance, we held a community conversation. Social Presencing Theater began as an event for an organization or community (a social system). A theater performance began the event. The performance was created from interviews with members of that social system. The following open conversation was a reflection and resonance process. In some cases we designed a commitment-to-action ritual at the end.

In 2008, after Gregor Barnum, Otto, and I began discussing what Social Presencing Theater was and what it could be used for, Gregor, my son Kobun Kaluza, Beth Mount, Greg Pierotti, Nicole Vidor, and I set out to make something with Otto's ideas. As an aside, this is often how the process goes: Otto has an idea (I hardly ever have ideas), and a team made up of whoever happens to be around at the time goes off and makes something that gets iterated (usually not sufficiently) before we try it out in a program or at an event. This team created several community Social Presencing Theater performances that triggered community conversation. Greg, an actor and writer with the Tectonic Theater Project shared a method for devising theater called Moment Work.[1] After we had completed our interviews, we used this method to create the fifteen-to-twenty-minute performances.

One event was for a Presencing Institute strategic planning meeting, another for a meeting on environmental sustainability for Sky Lake Meditation Center in New York. Penny Williamson and I held one with doctors and staff as part of an evaluation process on medical training for the Lehigh Valley Health Network in Pennsylvania. One event was with Beth Mount, artist, activist, and founder of Graphic Futures, and an organization in New York City called Job Path, which supports people with developmental disabilities. Our team, together with the Job Path community, created a performance for New York

City and New York state agencies. The performance triggered dialogues that supported agencies in their efforts to make innovations in care and housing. These events were part of a larger Theory U change initiative headed by Beth Mount and cited in the *Stanford Social Innovation Review*.[2]

What Is Social Art?

On the one hand, you could say that all of the performing arts are social art, in that they require social systems—teams, ensembles, troupes, crews, and audiences—to manifest. We are familiar with examples in which performance, film, and theater have provided a mirror to us as community to see ourselves at our best and our worst—the fullness of humanity. In the films of Iranian director Majid Majidi, the kora music of Malian Toumani Diabate, the plays of Black American playwright Ntozake Shange, I see and feel into the lives of others. We each live in our small microsystems that operate within our larger global ecosystem. But sensing the bigger context in which we live is difficult. The arts invite us into a larger perspective. We can sense our collective humanity as one living, breathing system. Deep sensing opens the door to understanding and to dialogue that can inspire, inform, activate and heal.

Some artists deliberately create work that addresses social issues. Over the past few decades, various kinds of theater designed to promote social change have been created. The most well known might be Theatre of the Oppressed, developed in the 1970s by Brazilian theater practitioner and political activist Augusto Boal.[3] Its methods are now practiced worldwide to address social inequality and oppression. Empatheatre is a powerful research-based theater-making methodology from South Africa that engages diverse communities on issues of race and power.[4] The Tectonic Theater Project in the United States created a groundbreaking play about homophobia and hate crimes with *The Laramie Project*.[5]

And there are many examples in the visual arts. The women of Gee's Bend, Alabama, quilted together to produce stunningly beautiful quilt art—a celebration of their community. Lily Yeh's mosaic mural projects empower communities and promote healing in the United States, Rwanda, and elsewhere. And there are many more examples. The intention of our work is to enable a social system, an organization or community, to sense itself—to feel its humanity and its own longing for health and well-being. We offer Social Presencing Theater to this ongoing stream of artistic work that responds to a need for deeper understanding of and compassionate engagement with our human condition.

Artistic expression can strengthen our confidence in human potential and has long been a catalyst for change. Art opens our hearts—our felt sense of connection to others and to creative possibilities. Although art always holds the potential for transformation for both the art maker and the receiver or viewer, social art emphasizes a societal vision of art—that every person is an artist in that they are creating social reality every day. Social art practices celebrate everyday living as a creative process and elicit our natural capacity for innovating and prototyping new ways of relating to today's challenges.

Visual artists Kelvy Bird, Olaf Baldini, and Jayce Pei Yu Lee are practitioners of another social art, called Generative Scribing, a process of graphically recording the spoken word that enables us to harvest learning and deepen our understanding of social fields and transformation of systems. Designer Ricardo Dutra and artist-activist Beth Mount produce artifacts, handmade objects that enhance understanding. Some of these are drawings, modeling clay figures, dioramas of futures we want to create, and souvenirs in clear plastic balls that capture our learning journey. Poets Manish Srivastava and John Stubley gather words and create poems that reflect our collective aspirations and heartbreaks. Social art often combines the disciplines of Social Presencing Theater, scribing, artifact making, and spoken word. Creative collaboration is an essential ingredient in the presencing transformation processes.

Social Field Resonance

Resonance is a word that oscillates between the subjective and objective. It is not cognitive alone but is a felt knowing and a shared knowing between the viewer and what is viewed. Resonance awakens a sense of aesthetics, an appreciation for the fullness of space and time. In 2017, Ricardo Dutra and I received funding from the Stuart Foundation to bring Social Presencing Theater into the Diego Rivera Learning Complex in South Central Los Angeles. At the school, we had an opportunity to make the first prototype of a Social Field Resonance process. The young people took Polaroid photos of their Stuck shapes and Sculpture 2 shapes. Ricardo photographed those images and then played them back as a slideshow for the students.

As each student saw the images, they spoke aloud what they had written about each one. At the end, there was silence in the room. There was a powerful sense of a collective experience, as though the social field itself had spoken. The students shared that they felt that their life situation was revealed in these sculptures, that everyone respected one another, and that they felt supported by knowing that others also were struggling. They felt seen and that their experience was of value. This experience made visible the change process of each student from

Stuck to Sculpture 2, their first-person experience; it also allowed them to sense their social field, their collective experience. Their artistic performance was not only powerful, showing the beauty and strength of each young person's sculpture and words; it also revealed the deeper layer of the social field and shed light on the profound sense of care that could become a catalyst for change.

Social Arts Studio Residency

In 2010 at the Presencing Masterclass, I met Claudia Madrazo, the remarkable Mexican arts and education innovator and founder of La Vaca Independiente. Since 2012, she has hosted Social Presencing Theater courses and gatherings in the Yucatan Peninsula that have enabled me to write and investigate Social Presencing Theater as social art. Gatherings of artists, naturalists, educators, and social change activists have included learning journeys into Mayan communities, workshops with young promoters of culture in the Mayan community, and the creation of performance work in collaboration with Mayan youth. Claudia's organization, La Vaca Independiente, has done remarkable work in Mexico to bring art into classrooms to support social-emotional learning through an innovative education program called dia (Development of Intelligence through Art).

In 2019, Ricardo Dutra and I collaborated with Claudia on the first Social Arts Studio Residency at an art installation hacienda in the Yucatan Peninsula. About twenty artists, educators, naturalists, and change-makers gathered to discuss social art. The group self-organized around four topics: traditional Mayan food; Mayan youth; creating a Social Presencing Theater performance; and creating programming for Hacienda Ochil, a cultural space in Merida. We went on learning journeys to local Mayan communities to hear stories about traditional life, about the natural habitat and farming, and about the young promoters of Mayan cultural traditions. From our interviews, a small group created a performance loosely using the Moment Work method that I had learned from Greg Pierotti. We used a variation on the Japanese poetry form haiku as a way to bring essential language into the performance.

In 2020, a diverse group gathered for the second Social Arts Studio Residency, and this time the focus was on co-creating a performance that would include Mayan young people from the local community of Izamal. Our group of adult visitors joined the La Vaca Independiente staff who worked with the young people aged thirteen to fifteen. In our studio space, we created a loose structure that this very diverse group of people could use to co-create the performance. The structure needed to allow enough space for people to settle into the natural beauty of the environment, to make spontaneous connections with one another, and to hold the contributions and inspiration of everyone, particularly the Mayan young people.

The structure also needed to hold a step-by-step process for creating a performance as the culmination of the nine-day residency. Most of the participants had no experience creating theater. In the first few days, the visitors and La Vaca staff engaged in the basics of Social Presencing Theater in the studio space. Then the team, headed by Laura Pastorini and Claudia, led a workshop with the young people. During the following days, the group created the performance material, loosely using the Moment Work process. We got feedback from the young people on what we had made and invited them to also make "moments." We integrated what they had created, arranged the parts in a logical order, rehearsed, and then adults and young people performed at the town plaza. After the performance, the young people and other performers sat in clusters with audience members to reflect on the experience.

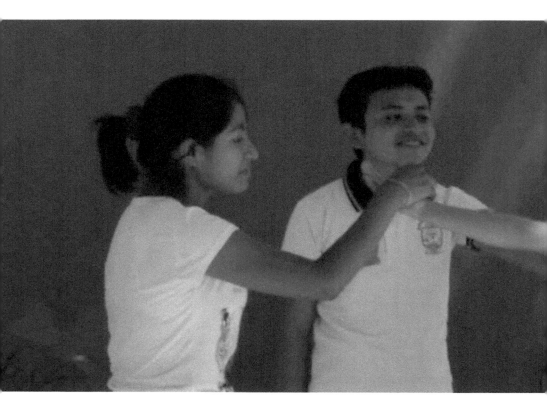

Figure 22: Social Art Residency in collaboration with La Vaca
Independiente, Mexico, 2020. Photo credit: Victor Rejón.

The elements of social art were present—co-creation, collaboration, inclusion, and an emphasis on a creative process based on mutual appreciation. We held the intention to deepen understanding and relationships across cultures, languages, and ages, and to make visible the genuine gifts and concerns of the Mayan young people. This experience deepened our sense of the potential for social art as an agent of profound social change.

We experienced these projects as examples of social art for several reasons. First, they were co-created, made collaboratively, and within a social context. The underlying assumption was that every person was creative and held a vital piece of the whole. In the social art process, participants could contribute movement, spoken words, music, visual art—the creative process was interdisciplinary.

Second, they had a shared intention to be of benefit to others. Third, the process of *making* the performance was just as valuable as the final product. The process was an expression of appreciation and had to include joy. And last, the performance mirrored back to us who we were as a community and society. The diversity of the social body placed our experience within a bigger picture than the local context. Both the performance and the process became triggers for reflection and dialogue.

Although these examples are of Social Presencing Theater as a performance event, most of our work has been and continues to be with individuals and small groups in organizational and social settings, using the practices described in this book. But whether it is Social Presencing Theater practices or Social Presencing Theater as a performance art, the process is the same: sensing into the context, co-creating an activity, engaging in a movement journey, witnessing with a resonance process, and applying learnings to the everyday work or life context. The creative process itself arises from the social field—the field of the collaborators and of the larger social context in which they operate. Then the performance becomes an invitation for the audience to sense into the larger social system of which we are all a part. The performance becomes a mirror for the community to see and sense itself.

12

ART AND RESEARCH

It might seem like an odd marriage—art and research. But this connection has grown quite organically within the Presencing Institute. Both art and research are based on an appetite for discovery. People possess an innate capacity to sense a social field. We are sensitive to our social surroundings, and we experience joy and inspiration when we are in settings that spark fresh ways of thinking and acting. Social fields are not foreign to us. However, this is a knowing that can be partially unconscious and can be brought further into our awareness, cultivated, and refined as a key factor in social change transformation. Published research on social fields can be an entry point for people in the same way that Jon Kabat-Zinn's research on mindfulness invited millions of people to engage in a practice that had previously been primarily associated with Asian spiritual practices.[1]

For the past few years, a group of Presencing Institute practitioner-researchers headed by Eva Pomeroy has begun to investigate social fields. The Social Presencing Theater practices are an innovative method for contributing to this effort. Neuroscientists, including Richard Davidson at the University of Wisconsin, Tanya Singer at the Max Planck Society in Germany, and others have used magnetic resonance imaging (MRI) and other neuroscience techniques to study the shifts that mindfulness and compassion practices have created in individuals, but there is no MRI or corresponding instrument for measuring shifts in social fields. The global ecological and social challenges present in today's world call for innovative methods, tools, and frameworks that bring the intelligence of the collective heart and body into the process of research. We join a new type of action research community whose work is based in awareness and whose work supports brave and compassionate action.

We know that the practices uncover insights and empower actions that transform work and life. This knowledge prompted us to ask questions, and those questions inspired our research. Most of this is future work, though we also feel an urgency to address our collective inability to find solutions to the global challenges. More knowledge about and clearer articulation of social fields can support the efforts of people engaged in awareness-based systems change. As data became available through stories, photos, and videos, we began to use the Social Presencing Theater practices as a research methodology to study what enables social systems to shift from a collection of individuals with self-interests to a generative, sustainable, and creative collective.

Ricardo Dutra heads the Social Presencing Theater research efforts on social field shifts for the Presencing Institute. The focus of our work is Sculpture 1, Sculpture

2, and the shift between Sculptures 1 and 2. The practices themselves are the embodied experience, the source of knowing, and data collection. Our questions and areas of interest have been quite specifically about patterns of stuck, awareness as the enabling condition for change, patterns of change, and a language that describes those patterns. Researchers with other interests are contributing to our collective understanding. Ninni Sodhal, Michael Stubberup, Andrea Chlopczik, and Agathe Peltereau-Villeneuve are engaged in research that looks at meditation and social fields.[2] Understanding and articulating field shifts more precisely could greatly benefit organizations and communities. We aspire to hold open space for researchers with different areas of interest and questions whose work would enrich all of our learning.

In addition to the practices themselves, reflective journaling, interviewing, and social resonance practice, Ricardo has introduced photographs, drawings, and video (visual language) to better understand stuck patterns and what ignites the creative capacity and wisdom of both individuals and social fields. When I looked at a photo image of my own stuck, I had an insight—how out of balance I looked—that had not arisen in my mind from embodying the stuck shape. When a team looked at a video of their group stuck, they clearly saw that their overfocus on the stuck person prevented them from experiencing where the whole system sculpture wanted to move. Seeing the image added another layer of useful information.

Our research has three areas of inquiry. We are looking at the ways individuals and social groups get disconnected from their own creative potential, and the conditions that enable forward movement. We ask whether there are archetypal patterns of stuck for individuals and systems. Second, how does collective awareness enable a system to shift? Third, can we develop a language to describe the patterns of movement from Sculpture 1 to Sculpture 2? The two visual prompts and tools described later in this chapter are early efforts to develop a shared language for describing the nuances of the shift from ego to ecosystem.

Patterns of Stuck

The Stuck practice is one method we have used to look at how individuals and systems lose touch with their ability to move forward and how they might shift toward sustainable innovation.[3] We began by looking at an individual's practice, positing that the body and mind are a system and that there may be patterns in the individual's process that parallel the social system process. Rather than looking at a system from the outside, we gather data by tracking the feeling quality in our individual body as it moves from Stuck to Sculpture 2, and by collecting the experiences of others in small teams who are witnessing the activity.

From engaging in and looking at the stuck shapes that individuals created, we began to notice patterns. Because the patterns were so recurrent, we called them archetypes. (We are not referring here to Jungian archetypes.) We noticed that the body shapes people created fell on a continuum. On one end were sculptures that expressed turning inward—often bending over, weighted down, or collapsed. They had no or limited vision and did not engage with their environment. On the other end were those with arms and legs stretched wide, overextended and pulled in multiple directions. These shapes communicated a loss of grounding and center. Between these are many other stuck shapes. For instance, there are some in which the face and arms reach forward while the lower body weight is pulled back. Or the body is twisted with one arm pulled forward and one to the back.

We noticed that there were parallels between the body shapes that individuals made and the social patterns that groups made when engaging in the Dance of Fives. In chapter eight we saw team patterns that were turned inward or scattered outward. We recognize that similar inhibiting patterns appear in the culture of organizations and larger social systems. There are many ways in which individuals and social systems experience stuckness, and in the past couple of years our research efforts have been focused on this continuum from closed to dispersed.

German artist and theorist Joseph Beuys illustrated his theory of sculpture, which was based on the inherent form of a plant. Beuys posited that the enabling conditions for a harmonious and healthy plant could be applied to all living organisms, including the social organism, the social system.

In the drawing entitled "evolution" Beuys laid a simple scale over the diagram against which we can assess the health of an organism: whether it has become too hardened and sclerotic or is in a state of dissolution; or if it is somewhere in the middle, harmonious and healthy, between the two extremes.[4]

At a research meeting, Otto Scharmer made a drawing on the board that seemed related to Beuys's diagram. On one end was a circle with arrows pointing into its center. This indicated a self-centralized archetype, perhaps a system that was overly fixated and "hardened," with no vision outward. (One example of this might be a hospital ward where staff focus on just their ward without sharing information or collaborating with others in the system.) At the other end he drew a collection of random shapes indicating action going in different directions with no coordinating mechanism, perhaps an image of "dissolution." (For example, in one group that I am currently in, each person is engaged in their own project, and there is not enough binding factor to hold the group together even though we have similar interests.) Then he drew a heart in the middle, which might have indicated the "harmonious and healthy" system. This led to our second area of research—what enables the field to shift.

Awareness as an enabling condition for change

Looking at the individual sculptures, we next asked what conditions enabled the individual to shift from stuck to a second sculpture that held some genuine information about next steps or emerging possibilities. We kept a record of our own experiences, observed others practicing, and attended to reflections shared by others. We noticed that when mindfulness grounded us in an embodied presence, we could easily connect with the knowledge held in the body. We noticed that when we held on to ideas about a desired outcome, there was limited learning and little sense of transformation. We identified "trust in the body" and "not knowing" as enabling conditions, and we noted that gleaning meaning from embodied experience and translating that into verbal language demanded accurate and subtle perception. When attending to the shift, we noted that identical Stuck shapes created by different people inevitably shifted into very different sculpture 2s— each revealing information needed by the practitioner.

Research on individual embodied transformation has provided a foundation as we turn our attention to the complexity of social body and social field transformation. In addition to the inner conditions present in individual practice, expanded awareness of the whole is a key component of social field practices such as group Stuck, the Village, and 4-D Mapping. Here we need methods for investigating the quality of the relationship field. By looking closely at the choices people make as they arrange themselves in an embodied social system, can we gain a deeper understanding of how groups can evolve into healthy and harmonious systems that are both grounded and contained, as well as open and expansive? When this balance occurs in the Social Presencing Theater practices, the group expresses warmth and inclusion, and also has the ability to innovate, contrast, differ, and explore. We see evidence of this but are at the beginning stages of our research.

Pattern language

There are many possible directions for research in this area, and we are beginning to explore the field of pattern language as a possible way to describe with nuance the transformation from Sculpture 1 to Sculpture 2. We need a language that can sharpen our perception of the movement and visual experience and enhance the felt knowing of that journey. To begin our research in this area, Ricardo and I developed the thirty-six aesthetic language cards (described in chapter nine) to enhance perception of and reflection on the three layers of experience—the physical-visual, the feeling quality of relationships, and awareness. Ricardo created visual symbols for each aspect to evoke a symbolic resonance. These reflection cards were our first step in developing a pattern language for social field shifts.

Having a language for speaking about experience supports the visibility of the transformation. The Stuck archetypes with visual images and the aesthetic language cards have introduced a fresh way to express a felt embodied experience—moving away from interpretation, memories of past experience, or emotional meaning. When participants used the cards they were able to attend to specific moments of experience and to stay longer in a process of suspension without immediately categorizing and overlaying conventional meaning on experience. This increased a nuanced sense of meaning. We also observe that having fresh language helps participants shift their attention from self-orientation to an awareness of the social body. Giving language to the felt dimension of experience heightened awareness in practitioners of themselves as co-creators of a system, rather than separate unrelated parts.

We are continuing our research on how language can support understanding of social field shifts by adapting the concept of a pattern language from the work of Christopher Alexander, emeritus professor of architecture at the University of California, Berkeley. In *A Pattern Language*, Alexander and colleagues describe pattern as a problem or issue that recurs in a particular context; and they describe the essence of a solution, leaving open any number of ways of moving to a solution.[5] Although we do not frame our work as a problem and solution, we do frame it as a stuck situation and a seed that holds potential for moving forward. In this way Alexander's description of a solution is resonant with our research frame: "the heart of the pattern—which describes the field of physical and social relationships which are required to solve the stated problem."[6] He describes design choices as ways of creating good human relationships and aliveness—what he called "the quality without a name."[7] The work of Professor Takashi Iba and his colleagues at Keio University in Japan on pattern language in human behavior also informs our work.[8] One next step might be to research a pattern language to describe the process of moving from a stuck situation into a future possibility.

Social Presencing Theater in Education

Education is a major acupuncture point for change. Ricardo Dutra's research is primarily in education. Colleagues Ingvild Øverland and Heather Huggins are engaged in research on Social Presencing Theater and learning environments. Ingvild works with children and teachers in both Norway and China.[9] Heather teaches theater with young recent immigrants in the New York City community college system. They and others contribute to the development of Social Presencing Theater as a research methodology in education.

In chapter eleven I spoke about our work in the Los Angeles Public School System. Ricardo, Adam Yukelson, and I offered workshops for teachers and also brought Social Presencing Theater practices to students at the Diego Rivera Learning Complex. At the end of our time there, we conducted interviews with the principal of one of the schools and with some of the students, using an adapted version of microphenomenology interviewing.

Microphenomenology is based on the work of biologist and neuroscientist Francisco Varela and now carried forward by researcher Claire Petitmengin. The interviewing method supports a person's ability to evoke and then describe minute details of their lived experience that usually would go unnoticed. It is difficult enough to attend with precision to what we notice, but even more challenging to attend to *how* we notice, or to the noticing itself.

Microphenomenology supports the Social Presencing Theater research processes that inquire into the shift from Stuck to moving and from ego orientation to ecosystem awareness.

Even the small number of interviews we were able to conduct at the Diego Rivera Learning Complex revealed some of the impact of our visits to the school. The principal spoke about the moment when she looked at the students' Stuck photos and words and felt the enormous pressure that she and the school system were putting on the students, who were already under tremendous stress from home lives of poverty and violence, the threat of deportation, struggles with the English language, and peer relationships. Although she was aware of the students' difficulties, she had a sudden felt experience of how severely the education system was failing them and the need for education to encompass more than simply academic achievement.

One student recounted a simple story about waiting for a job interview. He said that while he waited he was slumped over in his chair and jiggling his leg. Suddenly he remembered something from the workshop about embodying his Sculpture 2. He remembered the posture and the feeling of confidence he felt when he was in that posture. This memory made him sit up straight and helped him feel calmer and more settled. Another student said that his Stuck sculpture unlocked something for him, and that as a result he was trying to express himself more to his family and at school. These stories are not about massive systems change, but they reveal that small gestures performed and seen by others have the power to effect transformation.

Research Tools: The Postcard
and the Journey Map

The Postcard and Journey Map are two tools that increase our capacity to both better understand the journey from Sculpture 1 to Sculpture 2 and to articulate the change process with more precision. They were created as ways to collect data on the process and as instruments to help participants integrate their experience. They also offer us a way to think about measuring the impact of the practices on the creation of good learning environments.

Ricardo had developed a reflection protocol for the students, using Polaroid cameras. Students gathered in groups of five to reflect on where in their personal or

Figure 23: Postcard Gallery; postcard template (front and back). Design by Ricardo Dutra.

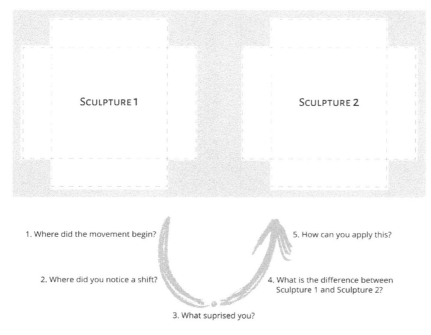

1. Where did the movement begin?

2. Where did you notice a shift?

3. What suprised you?

4. What is the difference between Sculpture 1 and Sculpture 2?

5. How can you apply this?

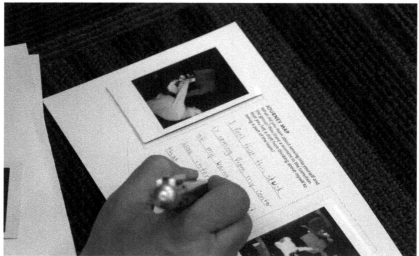

Figure 24: Journey Map and Journey Map template. Design by Ricardo Dutra.

school life they felt challenged or stuck. As each showed the body shape of their Stuck to the others, a group member took a Polaroid picture of their Stuck. Each student glued the photo to one side of a "postcard" that we provided. On the other side, they gave their Stuck a name, and then asked the Stuck to write them a message. They were asked to regard their stuck situation as a friend who wanted to help them. We asked, "What is it that the Stuck would like to tell you?" We asked them to begin the message with "Dear (name)," as they would do if writing to a friend.

The photographs, the names that they gave to the images, and the messages gave us a window into the stuck patterns of the students. We learned how much the students liked working with the cameras and how willing they were to share their challenges in small teams. The students benefited in several ways. In their small groups, the students reported that they realized they were not alone and that there was a way to share their issues with others and receive peer support. They said that the practice and the postcards allowed them to feel safe and to appreciate each other. They reported that they were not able to discuss personal issues with their families and did not want to go to the school guidance counselor. The practice presented another option for them. I described in chapter eleven the Social Field Resonance process that further enhanced the students' experience of the supportive social body and social field.

The Journey Map, first created for the students, gave us a more detailed set of data about the social body's movement from the Stuck group sculpture to Sculpture 2. One student took a picture of the group's Stuck and then took a second picture of their Sculpture 2—where the first sculpture moved to. These photos were glued onto a drawing of a U shape, and students responded to prompts that were written on the drawing. The Journey Map brought more awareness to the students engaged in the process, and they were able to articulate the details of their experience more clearly. They became aware that the whole system has to shift for transformation to occur, and that it is not up to the one stuck individual to make the changes alone. The prompts allowed us to look more closely at the field shift, compare responses, and look for patterns.

When dancers and designers create new ways to do action research and aesthetics play a major role, we know that we are not simply researching what is, but are researching what has not yet happened. We investigate not only to gain knowledge, but also to gain wisdom that can support the millions of people on the planet who aspire to create Beuys's harmonious and healthy system—a seeming impossibility in the midst of a pandemic, raging wildfires and storms, racial violence, economic inequality, escalating emotional stress, and political madness. We celebrate research that contributes to making the impossible possible.

EPILOGUE

ART AND EVERYDAY LIFE

Social Presencing Theater is not just about the practices. It is about a way of living in harmony with our experience. Each of us is an artist—a creative being—whether we engage in a formal art practice or not. Each of us is co-creating a life with others. We are interconnected. Each experience is the expression of interdependence. We are all engaged in the moment-to-moment business of creating social reality in our families, organizations, and communities. The everyday activity of creating society is a vast co-creation process in which there are no passive audience members. We are all creators and performers. This process manifests in each of us in the details of our daily life—in what we notice, where we put our attention, what choices we make. Artfulness is seeing the uniqueness in our everyday experience. We appreciate our ordinary daily activities—cooking dinner, answering emails, sitting on the bus. We are not at war with our life, continuously wishing it were different or dismissing moments of life as meaningless or not worthy of our attention. The everyday gestures and movements that arise from this place of appreciation and nonaggression are true moves. In this way, living is the creation of social art.

We cannot simply think our way out of the challenges we have on the planet today. We need all of our intelligences, including the sensing-body intelligence. Theory U suggests a way of living a creative life and of seeing the world as one living system. Social Presencing Theater connects body-knowing with heart-and-mind knowing in our work and daily life. Social Presencing Theater is an opportunity to reconnect with ourselves, synchronize body and mind, and to recognize our full humanness in the creative company of others. When we consider a broader definition of the word dance—some movement and some stillness in relationship to time and space— then everybody's nonverbal, spatial life is a dance. Each of our movements has power, beauty, and honesty. With a little attention to our physical bodies and to our social bodies, we can bring these qualities of power, beauty, and honesty to each of our true moves.

The body moves from one resting posture to another during the day. Its activities and relationships to others are constantly moving and changing. Social Presencing Theater investigates how we perceive and respond to change without having to control, avoid, or manipulate. Can we perceive and respond in fresh ways, without agendas, or are we trapped in conditioned and habitual patterns? The invitation is to engage with an open and curious mind. What is going to happen if I relax and let my body and the space lead me? In these practices there is no right or wrong outcome—only learning. Social Presencing Theater is an investigation of the relationship between mind, body, and the external world. Experiencing the practice is itself the learning.

Social Presencing Theater is at its root a Dharma Art. My teacher, Chögyam Trungpa, described Dharma Art as the practice of nonaggression. Art practices can be a bridge between a more formal meditation practice and everyday life experience. Social Presencing Theater is not "real life" exactly. It is an invitation to find the essential quality of experience—to bring the sacred and mundane together. In the process, perhaps we experience grace. A school leader in Hawaii expressed to me his aspiration that change could be "graceful." In this world of disruptive and violent shifts, the word *graceful* seemed out of place. And yet, when I tuned in to my sensing body, it welcomed this word. It softened me. Perhaps we underestimate the power of gracefulness and nonaggression. Perhaps this moment is full of grace, and we are just too busy, too afraid, too hell-bent on change to even notice.

The voice of urgency says there is no place for this kind of approach and language today. Social Presencing Theater begs to differ. Living without making war on this Earth and on others is the practice of art in everyday life. Each of us is an artist, and each of us co-creates this grand performance.

The foundation of this work is a strong conviction that human beings are basically good—basically wise and kind and brave. Throughout history, women and men have held a strong conviction that individual human beings and groups of human beings are basically good. Many today hold a strong aspiration that an emerging future, co-created by us all, could manifest this goodness in our global society. This view is not about morality or good versus bad. It expresses a conviction that all beings can access a purity of mind and heart. For ages, humans have worked together to create amazing things. We have extended ourselves in extraordinary ways to help others, and we have made the impossible possible. Wakeful and compassionate leaders have joined Heaven and Earth—

joined a vast vision with practical know-how—to bring forth the best in humanity. We can see the goodness in people every day in ordinary life. We experience this goodness in the simple presence and actions of people—in their openness, their intelligence, and their care. On any given day, there are moments of beauty and appreciation for being alive as human beings on this planet with other beings, human and nonhuman. Social Presencing Theater invites us to make the true moves that are ours to make to create a society of brilliance, warmth, and strength.

ACKNOWLEDGMENTS

Everything that I have done or made in my life has been due to the generosity and creative collaboration of others. There is no way I could include the names of all the teachers, colleagues, dance company members, collaborators, and friends who have contributed to the work described in this book. Reflecting on these many wonderful people has filled my heart with gratitude.

My first expression of gratefulness is to Chögyam Trungpa, Rinpoche, and to his son, Sakyong Mipham, Rinpoche, for their endless kindness to me and for their teaching on art as a vehicle for creating enlightened society, and to the Shambhala sangha that has been my training ground for nearly half a century. Any contribution that I may have made to the creation of Social Presencing Theater comes from the teachings of Shambhala.

Many people have requested, supported, encouraged, scolded, danced, and cajoled this book into being. But before I express my gratefulness to them, I need to say the names of a few of the many people who contributed to this work. Most of them did so decades before it emerged as Social Presencing Theater. I have been told that I am not the easiest person to work with, so these are the names of a few who stuck with me in spite of my bad habits. There are many more to whom I am indebted whose names I cannot include here.

After Jamie Cunningham asked me to dance the part of Hathor the cow at the 1968 American Dance Festival, I knew that one could be a professional dancer even if one were less birdlike and more cowlike. I am completely grateful for his guiding friendship as I began my journey.

Even though we long ago lost touch, I remember with gratitude the City Dance Theater dancers who traveled around Boston in the summer of 1972 on a mobile stage designed and built by my dear friend Janet Hurwitz: Idris Al-Sabry, Barbara Demps, Millard Hurley, and Jerry Puciato.

Great love and thanks go to Rylin Malone, Larry Teitelbaum, Robert Murphy, David Appel, Tom Krusinski, Raymond Allen, Judy Feldman, Michael Harris, Stan Strickland, and Carolyn Brown. This group of people shaped my life as an ensemble improviser. Many of us practiced the Village several times a week for several years—once all weekend without stopping. Some of us sold our belongings on the Cambridge Commons in the summer of 1974 and headed to Golden Gate Park, sleeping in the back yards of friends and family, performing in parks along the way.

So much gratitude goes to architect and designer Ed Howe, my partner in founding Jo Ha Kyu Performance

Group, who showed me the beauty of design with wooden 2-by-4s, bamboo, blue plastic tarps, and cloth. Some of those who joined us were Tom Krusinski, Scott de Lahunta, Alice Riccardi, Karin Ronning, Helena Chang, Norie Nishizawa, Ken Pierce, Olivier Besson, and Bart Uchida. I thank them for their loyalty and artistry.

One of my life's greatest blessings has been studying Japanese court dance and music with Suenobu Togi Sensei, and the many students in and out of Shambhala who came to study and perform with him, particularly Dessie Howard, Sarah Cox, Jim Wagner, Francesca Dalio, Chris Pleim, Bernie Kamps, and Chris Morel.

Much joyful gratitude to the team of brilliant improvisers who came together first at Naropa University and later at the Shambhala Institute for Authentic Leadership: Jerry Granelli, Lanny Harrison, Barbara Bash, and Steve Clorfeine. Making spontaneous performances, allowing expression to arise from nowness with these artists, was sheer delight.

If I had not met Otto Scharmer, who knows where I would be today—probably completely lost in European TV mysteries and crosswords. Every day I thank Heaven and Earth that he is on the planet, that auspicious coincidence brought us together, and that I have the opportunity to engage with him and the Presencing community in the emerging future. I am beyond grateful to him.

I also thank Peter Senge who has been a mentor, guide, and friend through these many years. Peter has had the most amazing way of offering critical feedback that sounds like praise.

All of our early understanding of how to make Social Presencing Theater was born with these co-creators: Kobun Kaluza, Greg Pierotti, Nicole Vidor, Joyce Rankin, Beth Mount, and Gregor Barnam. Although Gregor has passed away from his earthly body, his words, "We're just making this shit up," continue to be our creative process motto.

Much love and gratitude goes to Claudia Madrazo in Mexico, who has been my artistic sister and continues to inspire me to think big.

My friends Michael Stubberup and Nini Sodahl in Denmark have hosted me in their peaceful Danish setting for many years. The three-year Social Presencing Theater Masterclass provided the perfect container for deepening our understanding of the essence of the work.

I offer my heartfelt thank you to the Social Presencing Theater teachers, too many to name here, whose dedication and loyalty continues to hold the integrity of Social Presencing Theater. Kate Johnson, Manish Srivastava, Ricardo Dutra, Laura Pastorini, Mery Miguez, Daniela Ferraz, and Gene Toland taught Social Presencing Theater advanced programs with me, inspiring me and all of the students.

Thank you to all of the over 150 graduates of the Social Presencing Theater advanced programs, who brought commitment, intelligence, beauty, and depth to the co-creation and refinement of this work.

Thank you to all of the Social Presencing Theater practitioners, plus all my colleagues and faculty friends at the Presencing Institute, who have been endlessly supportive—Julie Arts, Marian Goodman, Beth Jandernoa, Katrin Kaeufer, Martin and Aggie Kalunda-Banda, Kelvy Bird, Antoinette Klatzky, Angela and Olaf Baldini, Manish Srivastava, Janice Spadafore, Dieter Van den Broeck, Laura Pastorini, Beth Mount, Anne-Sophie Dubanton, and so many more.

Nothing is possible without a core team, and I have the privilege of working with the very best, most joyful, most visionary and kind team who lead the global Social Presencing Theater engagement in social art, application, capacity building, and research: Manish Srivastava, Angela Baldini, Laura Pastorini, and Ricardo Dutra.

Now to the book itself. Two years ago, in Otto and Katrin's living room, Otto handed me an outline written on a napkin and said, "Here, this can get you started." Without Katrin's guidance and comments on the manuscript and Otto's text messages every few months asking "How's the book progressing?," this book would never have been written.

Georg Senorer offered his home in Italy as a writing retreat. Anders Fabricius suggested I start by writing postcards, brief jottings. Anna Whaley compiled the "nuggets" (themes and principles) that Kate Johnson and Manish Srivastava collected.

After I began writing and looking through my journal notes, Adam Yukelson worked with me for several months to get a structure. I am completely indebted to him for his support. It was his idea to devote a chapter to each practice and then to write a commentary on the practice.

Readers of early drafts whose insightful comments helped shape this book were Kelvy Bird, Andrea Chlopczik, Gaylon Ferguson, Noel Hayashi, Richard Reoch, and Jude Robison. Their support buoyed me through my early stumblings. Thanks to Beth Mount for incredibly careful reading and comments and to Kelly Notaras for a helpful consultation. My old friends Mary Lang and Janet Hurwitz shared their insights on images and design. The encouragement, precision, and suggestions made by all of these wonderful readers were key.

Many thanks to Emily Bower who edited earlier versions of the manuscript, smoothing bumpy places, keeping me out of the jargon weeds, and always encouraging.

Kelvy Bird and Katrin Kaeufer at PI Press made invaluable suggestions on later drafts, cheered me on, and shepherded the production of the book to its completion. Kelvy also contributed a drawing, as did Agathe Peltereau-Villeneuve. Much appreciation to them.

Thank you to Janet Mowery for her kindness and exquisite final editing and to Emma Dolores Paine for the endnotes. Both were a complete joy to work with. And thank you to Sarina Bouwhuis for reading the galley proofs with her usual care.

Ricardo Dutra and I spent several years traveling, making things up, trying things out, designing things and processes, researching. We had what I would call successes and failures. But for Ricardo, there was no such thing as success or failure, only learning. I am not a researcher, but Ricardo told me that living is researching. He designed this book. I cannot express enough how much I appreciate working with him on this journey.

My partner Gaylon helped turn my ramblings into prose and cheered me on when I was ready to press delete on the whole manuscript. His note "Off to a good start" on what I thought was a near final draft made me realize what hard work writing is. His graceful and penetrating writing is an inspiration.

My full-hearted gratitude to the entire extended Hayashi-Teitelbaum-Kaluza-Hoops-Redman-Gotesman-Ferguson-Ryan family. Ayla and Kobun have had to put up with my preoccupation with work since they were born. They and their splendid partners, Garrick and Mindy, and my grandchildren Asher, Beatrice, and Opal, are my constant joy and support. Kobun and I have been making work together in the theater since he was eight or nine years old. He was a koken in some of my earlier dances (a person who enters the stage in Japanese theater to rearrange the set, unremarked by the performers), and we made performance work together when he was in high school. He has been a Social Presencing Theater collaborator since we began. At times over the decades I have thought that he was the only person on the planet who had any idea what I was trying to do with my work.

NOTES

Prologue

1. Chögyam Trungpa, *True Perception: The Path of Dharma Art 1* (Boston: Shambhala Publications, 2008).

2. See C. Otto Scharmer, *Theory U: Leading from the Future as It Emerges* (San Francisco: Berrett-Koehler, 2009).

Chapter one

1. David I. Rome, *Your Body Knows the Answer: Using Your Felt Sense to Solve Problems, Effect Change, and Liberate Creativity* (Boston: Shambhala Publications, 2014).

2. Scharmer, *Theory U*, 352.

3. Henri Bortoft, *Taking Appearance Seriously: The Dynamic Way of Seeing in Goethe and European Thought* (Edinburgh: Floris Books, 2012), 15.

4. Chögyam Trungpa, *Shambhala: The Sacred Path of the Warrior* (Boston: Shambhala Publications, 1984), 84.

5. Chögyam Trungpa, *True Perception,* 25.

6. C. Otto Scharmer, *The Essentials of Theory U* (Oakland, CA: Berrett-Koehler, 2018).

7. Scharmer, *The Essentials of Theory U*, 25, 28, 30, 31.

8. Scharmer, *The Essentials of Theory U*, 29–32.

9. Trungpa, *True Perception*, 30.

Chapter two
   1. Scharmer, *Theory U*.

   2. Scharmer, *The Essentials of Theory U*, xi, 7, 28.

   3. Scharmer, *The Essentials of Theory U*, 26.

   4. MITx, "u.lab: Leading from the Emerging Future," https://l5www.edx.org/course/ulab-leading-fromthe-emerging-future.

Chapter three
   1. Steen Hildebrandt and Michael Stubberup, *Sustainable Leadership: Leadership from the Heart* (Copenhagen: Copenhagen Press, 2012), chapter 7.

   2. "Case Clinic," and "Case Clinic Toolkit," Presencing Institute, accessed October 13, 2020. https://www.presencing.org/resource/tools/case-clinic-desc.

   3. Chögyam Trungpa, *True Perception*, 30.

   4. Chögyam Trungpa, *The Future Is Open: Good Karma, Bad Karma, and Beyond Karma* (Boulder, CO: Shambhala Publications, 2018), 6.

   5. International Labour Organization, "Forced Labour, Modern Slavery and Human Trafficking," https://www.ilo.org/global/topics/forced-labour/lang--en/index.htm. See also International Labour Organization, *Profits and Poverty: The Economics of Forced Labour* (Geneva: ILO, 2014).

   6. Allen Ginsberg, "Mind Writing Slogans," *Poetry Ireland Review* 43/44 (1994): 17–20.

Chapter four
   1. The statement is attributed to Lewin in Charles W. Tolman, *Problems of Theoretical Psychology* (York, Ontario, Canada: Captus Press, 1995), 31.

2. Presencing Institute, "Awareness-Based Systems Change: Deep Resonance," *Field of the Future Blog*, June 24, https://medium.com/presencing-institute-blog/awareness-based-systems-change-deepresonance-bef9ca451749.

3. Senge is quoted in C. Otto Scharmer, *The Essentials of Theory U* (Oakland, CA: Berrett-Koehler, 2018), 62–63.

4. Robin Duval, "How Could Regeneration Increase Social Equality in Govanhill—A Systems Mapping Event Using Social Presencing Theatre," *Firestarter Festival Blog*, September 14, 2020, https://firestarterfestivalcom/2020/09/14/how-could-regeneration-increase-so ial-equality-in-govanhill-asystems-mapping-event-using-social-presencing-theatre/.

5. On mental models, see Peter M. Senge, *The Fifth Discipline: The Art and Practice of the Learning Organization* (United States: Crown, 2010), 163–164.

6. Duval, *Firestarter Festival Blog*, September 14, 2020.

7. A more thorough explanation of the tools associated with 4-D Mapping can be found in "Tools: 4D Mapping," Presencing Institute, accessed October 13, 2020, https://www.presencing.org/resource/tools/4D-mapping-desc.

8. Scharmer, *The Essentials of Theory U*, 43, 46–47.

Chapter five

1. David Chadwick, ed., *Zen Is Right Here: Teaching Stories and Anecdotes of Shunryu Suzuki* (Boston: Shambhala, 2007), 1.

2. See Bessel A. van der Kolk, *The Body Keeps the Score: Brain, Mind, and Body in the Healing of Trauma* (New York: Penguin Books, 2015); Peter A. Levine and Ann Frederick, *Waking the Tiger: Healing Trauma: The Innate Capacity to Transform Overwhelming Experiences* (Berkeley, CA: North Atlantic Books, 1997); Resmaa Menakem, *My Grandmother's Hands: Racialized Trauma and the Pathway to Mending our Hearts and Bodies* (Las Vegas: Central RecoveryPress, 2017).

3. Scharmer, *Essentials of Theory U*, 23–24.

Chapter six

1. Richard B. Pilgrim, "*Ma*: A Cultural Paradigm," *Chanoyu Quarterly* 46 (1986): 32–53.

2. Sen Soshitsu XV, "*Ma*: A 'Usefully Useless' Thing," *Chanoyu Quarterly* 46 (1986): 5.

3. Sen Soshitsu XV, "*Ma*: A 'Usefully Useless' Thing," 6.

4. Pilgrim, "*Ma*: A Cultural Paradigm," 34.

5. Pilgrim, "*Ma*: A Cultural Paradigm," 38.

6. Scharmer, *The Essentials of Theory U*, 43.

7. Jiddu Krishnamurti, "Saanen 1st Public Talk, July 10, 1966," in *Texts and Talks of Jiddu Krishnamurti*, July 10 1966, accessed October 13, 2020, http://jiddu-krishnamurti.net/en/1966/1966-07-10-jiddu-krishnamurti-1st-public-talk.

Chapter seven

1. Bruce W. Tuckman and Mary Ann C. Jensen, "Stages of Small-Group Development Revisited," *Group and Organization Studies* 2, no. 4 (1977): 419–427.

Chapter eight

1.

1. Edward Twitchell Hall, *The Hidden Dimension* (Garden City, NY: Doubleday, 1966).

Chapter nine

Scharmer, *The Essentials of Theory U*, 14.

2. Scharmer, *The Essentials of Theory U*, 34.

3. Quoted in Gia Kourlas, "Bill T. Jones Knows Life Will Change, and His Art, Too," *New York Times*, May 20, 2020.

Chapter ten

1. Lee Worley, *Coming from Nothing: The Sacred Art of Acting* (Boulder, CO: Turquoise Dragon Press, 2001).

Chapter eleven

1. Moisés Kaufman and Barbara Pitts McAdams, *Moment Work: Tectonic Theater Project's Process of Devising Theater* (New York: Vintage Books, 2018), 259–269.

2. Joanna Levitt Cea and Jess Rimington, "Creating Breakout Innovation," *Stanford Social Innovation Review* (Summer 2017): 38.

3. Augusto Boal, *Theatre of the Oppressed* (London: Pluto Press, 1979).

4. "Empatheatre," accessed October 13, 2020, https://www.empatheatre.com.

5. *The Laramie Project*, The Tectonic Theater Project, accessed October 13, 2020, https://www.tectonictheaterproject.org/?avada_portfolio=laramie.

Chapter twelve
1. Jon Kabat-Zinn, *Mindfulness for Beginners* (Boulder, CO: Sounds True, Inc., 2012); Jon Kabat-Zinn, Full Catastrophe Living (New York: Random House, 1990).

2. Andrea Chlopczik, "Conscious Change, Change in Consciousness: Prototyping Our Interior Condition," in *From the Edge of Chaos: Dialogues amongst Social Theory and Practice* (Bangalore: IBA Publications, 2016), 48–57; Steen Hildebrandt and Michael Stubberup, *Sustainable Leadership: Leadership from the Heart* (Copenhagen: Copenhagen Press, 2012).

3. "Tools: Stuck Exercise," Presencing Institute, https://www.presencing.org/resource/tools/stuckexercise-desc. See also Arawana Hayashi and Ricardo D. Goncalves, "A Pattern Language for Social Fields," *Journal of Awareness-Based Systems Change* (forthcoming 2021).

4. Volker Harlan, ed., *What Is Art? Conversation with Joseph Beuys* (United Kingdom: Rudolf Steiner Press, 2012), 3.

5. Christopher Alexander, *A Pattern Language: Towns, Buildings, Construction* (New York: Oxford University Press, 1977).

6. Alexander, *A Pattern Language*, xi.

7. Alexander, *A Pattern Language*, 19.

8. Takashi Iba, "Pattern Language 3.0 and Fundamental Behavioral Properties," in Peter Baumgartner, Tina Gruber-Muecke, and Richard Sickinger, eds., *Pursuit of Pattern Languages for Societal Change. Designing Lively Scenarios in Various Fields.* (Berlin: epubli, 2016), 200–233.

9. Ingvild Øverland, "Students' Experience with Social Presencing Theater and How This Can Facilitate Deeper Learning Processes" (master's thesis, University of Stavanger, 2019) (in Norwegian).

About the Author

Arawana's pioneering work as an innovator, performer, and educator is deeply sourced in both improvisation and the ancient Japanese court dance, Bugaku. She currently heads the creation of Social Presencing Theater for the Presencing Institute. She brings her background in dance and meditation to the creation of a movement practice that makes visible both current reality and emerging future possibilities. She teaches meditation and creative process in Shambhala, a community committed to the creation of enlightened society.

Figure 25: Arawana Hayashi and Otto Scharmer, 2017.
Photo credit: Aaron Kotowski, Strategy+Business magazine.

CPSIA information can be obtained
at www.ICGtesting.com
Printed in the USA
BVHW090808030321
601532BV00003B/11